THE
TECHNICAL
ANALYSIS
COURSE

THIRD EDITION

THE TECHNICAL ANALYSIS COURSE

A WINNING PROGRAM FOR INVESTORS & TRADERS

THOMAS A. MEYERS

MCGRAW-HILL

NEW YORK   CHICAGO   SAN FRANCISCO   LISBON
LONDON   MADRID   MEXICO CITY   MILAN   NEW DELHI
SAN JUAN   SEOUL   SINGAPORE   SYDNEY   TORONTO

The McGraw·Hill Companies

Library of Congress Cataloging-in-Publication Data

Meyers, Thomas A.
    The technical analysis course : a winning program for investors & traders / Thomas A. Meyers. — Rev. ed.
        p.   cm.
    ISBN 0-07-138710-2 (hardcover : alk. paper)
    1. Investment analysis. 2. Stocks—Charts, diagrams, etc. I. Title.
    HG4529 .M453   2002
    332.63'2042—dc21   2002006719

1 2 3 4 5 6 7 8 9 0   AGM/AGM   0 8 7 6 5 4 3 2

ISBN 0-07-138710-2

This publication is designed to provide accurate and authoritative information in regard to the subject matter covered. It is sold with the understanding that neither the author nor the publisher is engaged in rendering legal, accounting, or other professional service. If legal advice or other expert assistance is required, the services of a competent professional person should be sought.

—From a Declaration of Principles jointly adopted by a Committee of the American Bar Association and a Committee of Publishers

McGraw-Hill books are available at special quantity discounts to use as premiums and sales promotions, or for use in corporate training programs. For more information, please write to the Director of Special Sales, Professional Publishing, McGraw-Hill, Two Penn Plaza, New York, NY 10121-2298. Or contact your local bookstore.

 This book is printed on recycled, acid-free paper containing a minimum of 50% recycled de-inked fiber.

CONTENTS

CONTENTS

How to Take This Course

The objective of this course is to teach you technical analysis techniques that will enable you to preserve capital and boost investment profits, while at the same time minimizing risk of losses. It consists of text material for you to read and quizzes to complete. The quizzes are designed to reinforce the concepts brought out in the text portion and to enable you to evaluate your progress.

I recommend that you work at this course systematically. Only by reading the text and taking the quizzes at a regular and steady pace will you get the most out of this course and retain what you have learned.

The Text

The most important component of this course is the text. It is here that the concepts and techniques of technical analysis are first presented.

Reading each lesson twice will increase the likelihood of your understanding the text fully. In your first reading, concentrate on getting an overview of the lesson's contents. Pay attention to the headings and subheadings. Find the general theme of each section and see how that theme relates to others. Don't let yourself get bogged down with details during the first reading. Simply concentrate on remembering and understanding the major themes.

In your second reading, look for the details that underlie the themes. Read the entire lesson carefully and methodically, underlining key points, working out the details of the examples, and making marginal notations as you go.

The Quizzes

After reading a lesson and before going on to the next, work through the quiz at the end of the lesson. Answering the questions and comparing your own answers to those given will assist you in grasping the major ideas of that lesson. If you perform these self-check exercises conscientiously, you will develop a framework in which to place material presented in later lessons. This building process will help clarify the reading and, most important, will help you to apply what you have learned under real market conditions.

The Lessons

Similar to a carpenter, the technician has a variety of tools in his or her toolbox. Some basic tools (like bar charts and moving averages) are used quite frequently, while other more specialized and sophisticated tools (like relative strength index and stochastics) are used less often. Like a carpenter, each technician has his or her favorite tools, those which have been mastered through experience over time.

Each lesson in this course builds on the prior ones, providing you with the tools you need, from basic to complex, to become a master technician. Lesson 1 introduces you to technical analysis and explains the principles on which it is based. Lessons 2 through 18 teach you how to construct charts, spot profitable chart patterns, and use a variety of basic and advanced technical analysis tools. Finally, the last lesson (Lesson 19) pulls all the pieces together by, (1) showing you how to use a weight of evidence approach to technical analysis and, (2) providing three comprehensive real market examples.

For your benefit, recommended technical analysis books for further study are detailed in the appendix. In addition, key terms used throughout this course are defined in the glossary.

INTRODUCTION

THE PHILOSOPHY OF TECHNICAL ANALYSIS

Those "in the know" on Wall Street have increasingly turned to technical analysis in recent years. They realize that security prices do not move randomly, rather they move in repeating and identifiable patterns. They use this information to gain an edge on other investors and make money in the stock market. This course will enable others to do the same by making profitable investment decisions based on proven technical analysis techniques.

The Basic Principles

Before learning about the specific tools and techniques the technician (as one who employs technical analysis is called) uses to analyze various investment opportunities, it is essential that one understand the principles upon which technical analysis is based. The three key principles are:

1. Everything is discounted and reflected in market prices.
2. Prices move in trends and trends persist.
3. Market action is repetitive.

Let's examine each principle in detail.

The first and most important principle is that everything is discounted and reflected in market prices. The technician believes that all knowledge, regardless of type (fundamental, economic, political, psychological, or other), is already reflected in market prices. Technicians, unlike fundamental analysts, feel it is futile to study company financial statements, earnings and dividend reports, industry developments, and other data in an attempt to determine the "intrinsic value" of a stock or other market instrument since it is commonplace to have a wide divergence between the intrinsic value and actual market price. For example, it is not unusual for a company's stock to be trading at a price well above or below its book value per share. Technicians believe that the real value of a share of stock or other market instrument at any point in time is determined solely by supply and demand as reflected in trading activity.

Price movements are simply the reflection of changes in supply and demand. The technician does not care what the underlying forces of a shift in supply and demand are, rather he or she is interested in what occurs. If demand is greater than supply, prices will increase. On the other hand, if supply is greater than demand, prices will decline. *The study of market prices is all that is necessary.*

TECHNICAL ANALYSIS TIP

There is an old saying on Wall Street that goes "Sell on good news." Why should you sell on good news? Because if the actual news is as expected, it is, of course, already discounted and reflected in the market price. Therefore, you would expect no further rise in price based on that news.

The second principle on which technical analysis is based is that prices move in trends and trends persist. The supply and demand balance sets a trend in motion. Once in motion, a trend remains intact until it ends. For example, if a stock's price is moving up, it will continue its rise until there is a clear reversal. Likewise, if a stock is moving down, it will decline until a reversal.

An analogy will further clarify the second principle. When a car is parked in a garage, it is, in essence, trendless because it is not moving in a given direction. Assume a car is driven on to a street moving northbound. When the driver first turns on to that street, he or she is moving slowly but gradually picks up speed until a speed of 50 miles per hour is reached. The direction or trend is northbound. In order to change direction (or trend) to southbound, the driver would first have to slow down from 50 miles per hour, to perhaps five miles per hour, and turn around (or, perhaps, stop and drive in reverse). The driver could not instantly change direction (or trend), and if someone was following, this following motorist would be signaled by the slowing down before the first driver reversed direction (or trend).

Market prices move in a similar manner. First, they begin in one direction, up or down, creating a trend. That trend persists until the price movement slows and gives warning before finally reversing and moving in the opposite direction. At that point a new trend is initiated. As illustrated in Figure 1-1, trends can be readily spotted on charts. The chart patterns show the balance of supply and demand for a particular stock or other market instrument.

TECHNICAL ANALYSIS TIP

The old Wall Street adage "the trend is your friend" is true because, once begun, a trend is likely to continue. By following it you increase your probability of making money.

The final key principle on which technical analysis is based is that market action is repetitive. Certain patterns appear time after time on charts. These patterns have meanings that can be interpreted in terms of probable future price movement. Although not infallible, the odds are in their favor.

Human nature is such that it tends to react to similar situations in consistent ways. As a rule, people will act the same as they have in the past. Since the stock market is a reflection of the actions of people, technicians study it to determine how people will react under certain conditions and, thus, how security prices will move. Technicians analyze the recurrence of similar characteristics in an attempt to identify major market tops and bottoms.

Technical Analysis Defined

Giving consideration to the principles discussed, technical analysis can be defined as simply the study of individual securities and the overall market based on supply and demand. Technicians record, usually in chart form, historical price and volume activity and deduce from that pictured history the probable future trend of prices.

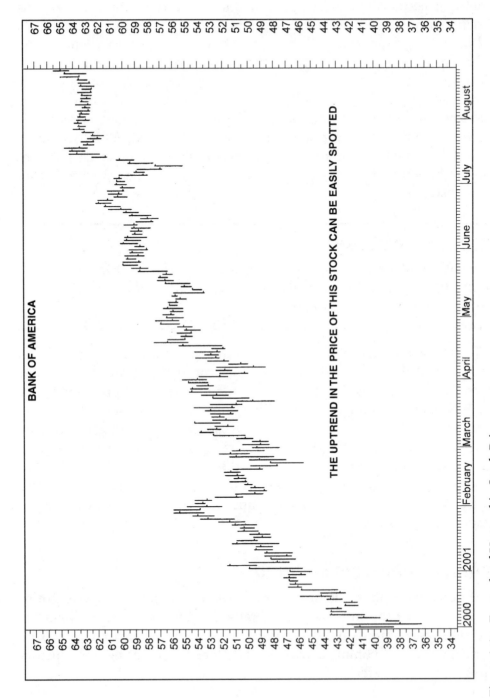

Figure 1-1   Example of Uptrend in Stock Prices

Adaptability to Different Markets and Investment Time Horizons

The beauty of technical analysis is that it can be applied effectively to virtually any trading medium and investment time horizon. A technician can analyze stocks, bonds, options, mutual funds, commodities, and many other forms of investments for buy and sell opportunities. And one can do so by examining tic-by-tic, intraday, daily, weekly, monthly, or some other interval of data to use technical analysis for a wide range of time horizons—from very short-term to very long-term perspectives.

The best manner in which to use technical analysis depends on one's approach to the market. Keep in mind that everyone invests differently. We all have different levels of stress, different temperaments, and different amounts of capital. It is important to apply technical analysis in a manner that complements one's own personality and individual investment philosophy. Obviously, those whose time, nerves, and capital are limited will want to pass up very short term trading opportunities (such as intraday trading of stock index futures) and, perhaps, use longer-term technical analysis derived buy and sell signals for stocks or mutual funds. By recognizing one's individual investment strengths and weaknesses, users of technical analysis can find the trading medium and time horizons that are best for their individual investment situations.

True or False Quiz

Circle **T** if the statement is true or **F** if the statement is false.

T
F
1.
Technicians study company financial statements and earnings and dividend reports to determine the value of a stock.

T
F
2.
Technicians believe that supply and demand determine the real value of a share of stock at any point in time.

T
F
3.
Technicians believe that the study of market prices is all that is necessary.

T
F
4.
Prices move in trends and trends persist.

T
F
5.
Trends in price typically change direction (either from up to down or down to up) without warning.

T
F
6.
Trends can easily be identified on charts.

T

F

7.

Market action is random in nature.

T

F

8.

Technical analysis can be applied to stocks, but not commodities.

T

F

9.

Technical analysis works better for short-term than long-term analysis.

Answers

1. *False.* Technicians believe it is futile to study fundamental data since it is already reflected in the market price of a stock.
2. *True.*Supply and demand, as reflected in actual trades typically made at a stock exchange, determine the market price (real value) of a company's stock at a given point in time.
3. *True.* Market prices reflect the supply and demand balance based on how investors act in certain situations.
4. *True.* This is the second principle upon which technical analysis is based.
5. *False.* Typically, prices moving either up or down will first decelerate the movement in the direction of the trend and then give warning prior to changing direction. Rarely does a trend reverse instantly.
6. *True.* See Figure 1-1 for an example.
7. *False.* Market action is repetitive and prices act in consistent ways under similar situations.
8. *False.* Technical analysis can be applied effectively to virtually any trading medium.
9. *False.* Although technical analysis is more often applied to short-term investment time horizons, it is equally effective in analyzing long-term trends.

CONSTRUCTING CHARTS

BASIC CHART CONSTRUCTION

As shown in Lesson 1, technicians do not believe that the price of securities and the overall stock market move in a random manner. Rather, they contend that a direct relationship exists between price movements in the past and those that will occur in the future. Their objective is to determine what this relationship is so that they will be able to predict accurately whether the stock market or a particular security's price will go up or down.

The primary tool that a technician uses is a "picture" or chart of a security's price movement.

Types of Charts

Technicians use four types of charts as illustrated in Figure 2-1. They are:

1. Bar chart.
2. Line (or close-only) chart.
3. Point and figure chart.
4. Japanese candlestick chart.

Bar charts are, by far, the most commonly used type of price chart. In a bar chart, a vertical line that ranges from the period's lowest price to its highest price represents each time period. A horizontal protrusion to the right marks the period's closing price.

Some technicians believe that the closing price is the most important price of the trading day and, therefore, plot only closing prices in a line chart.

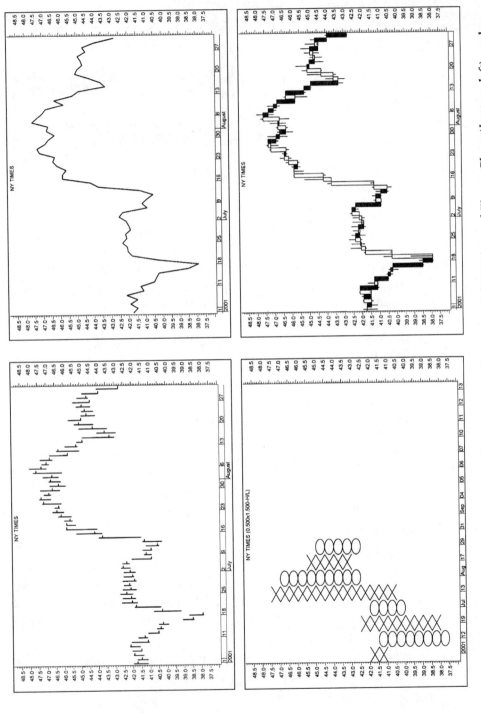

Figure 2-1 Comparison of Bar Chart (*top left*), Line Chart (*top right*), Point and Figure Chart (*bottom left*), and Japanese Candlestick Chart (*bottom right*)

The third type of chart, the point and figure chart, will be examined in depth in Lesson 17. For now, note that it shows the same price information as the bar and line charts, but in a more compressed fashion. A rising price change is represented by an X, a declining movement by an O. Each X or O occupies a box on the chart and represents a price change of a certain magnitude.

The final type of chart, the Japanese candlestick chart, is so called because the lines resemble candles and wicks. For each period, the opening, high, low, and closing prices are plotted in a manner that will be explained fully in Lesson 18.

Regardless of the type of chart used, the length of the period examined will vary depending on whether one is oriented to short-term, intermediate-term, or long-term investments. Although there is no generally accepted definition of these three terms, short-term roughly refers to the next three months; intermediate-term is about three to six months from the present time; and long-term is considered to be approximately six months to one year from the current period. Technicians often use hourly and daily charts to determine the short-term trend of security price movements. They use weekly charts for gaining an intermediate-term perspective. And, monthly and yearly charts help technicians examine the long-term.

As noted earlier, bar charts are the most common type of chart used by technicians. Let's examine the bar chart in more detail.

The Bar Chart

Constructing a bar chart is easy as shown in Figure 2-2. A price scale is assigned to the vertical axis; a time scale (hourly, daily, weekly, etc.) is marked off on the horizontal axis. For each period, the high, low, and closing prices are plotted. Usually, opening price is also plotted for commodities but not for stocks. A vertical line, or bar, connects the high and low prices. Horizontal tics to the left and right of the bar represent the opening and closing prices, respectively.

Let's look at a more comprehensive example. Assume a stock traded at the prices shown in Table 2-1 over a period of five weeks (25 trading days). A daily bar chart of these prices is provided in Figure 2-3. A weekly bar chart (see Figure 2-4) of the same prices is simply a condensed version of the daily chart with each bar representing five days of price activity.

Figure 2-2 How a Bar Chart Is Constructed
A: The high price for the day, $25.80
B: The low price for the day, $25.20
C: The opening price (not always on the bar chart), $25.30
D: The closing price, $25.70

TECHNICAL ANALYSIS TIP

A telephoto-type effect can be produced by viewing monthly, weekly, and daily bar charts in combination. First, look at a bar chart plotting monthly data to gain a long-term perspective. Then, examine a bar chart of weekly data to determine the intermediate-term trend. Finally, a chart of daily data gives a short-term picture. Many technicians use this total picture to improve their probability of making profits by only making short-term trades in the direction of the intermediate and long-term trends.

Table 2-1   Data for Bar Chart Example

Date	High	Low	Close
February 22	115.62	113.12	115.25
February 23	115.87	114.37	115.37
February 24	116.75	114.75	116.12
February 25	117.87	114.12	114.50
February 26	115.75	114.12	115.75
February 29	117.75	114.75	117.50
March 1	118.37	116.25	117.00
March 2	118.37	116.87	117.25
March 3	117.25	115.75	116.50
March 4	117.50	115.25	116.87
March 7	117.50	116.12	117.25
March 8	118.62	117.25	117.62
March 9	117.75	116.25	116.62
March 10	116.50	113.62	113.75
March 11	115.50	112.37	115.50
March 14	115.75	114.50	115.50
March 15	115.37	113.62	114.00
March 16	115.37	113.37	115.25
March 17	115.50	113.75	114.87
March 18	114.62	113.25	114.25
March 21	114.00	112.75	113.75
March 22	114.25	113.12	113.12
March 23	113.37	111.25	111.62
March 24	110.50	109.37	109.75
March 25	110.37	106.50	107.00

Arithmetic versus Logarithmic Scale

The vertical price scale on a bar chart can be arithmetic or logarithmic. Each type has advantages and disadvantages. However, no consensus opinion exists among technicians as to which is best.

First, let's examine how the two scales differ. On an arithmetic scale, an equal distance for each price unit of change is shown on the vertical scale. Thus, the distance between 10 and 20 on the vertical scale equals the distance between 20 to 30, 30 to 40, and so on. On a logarithmic scale, the

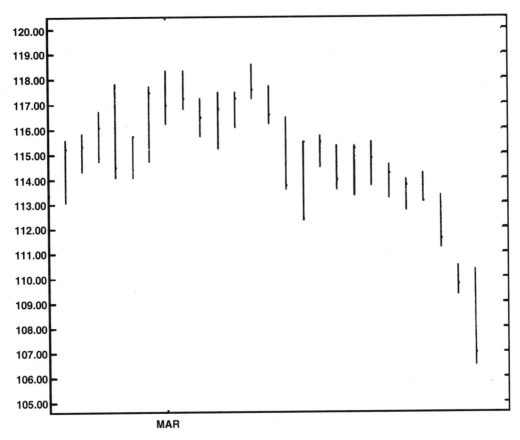

Figure 2-3   Daily Bar Chart

distance between each price unit of change represents an equal percentage change. For example, the difference between 10 to 20 and 40 to 80 is the same because each represents a 100 percent increase.

Figure 2-5 shows a comparison of arithmetic and logarithmic scales. Since chart patterns appear much the same on both scales, the type of vertical scale you use is up to personal preference. For consistency, the arithmetic scale will be used on charts throughout the remainder of this course.

Volume

The volume of trading activity for each time period is normally shown at the bottom of a standard bar chart. Each period's (day's, week's, etc.) volume is recorded by a vertical bar directly below that period's price bar.

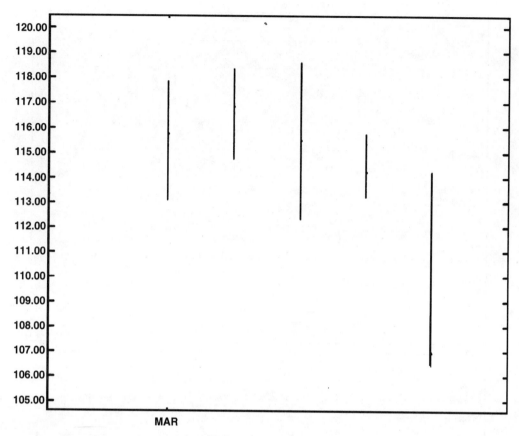

Figure 2-4   Weekly Bar Chart

The higher the bar, the higher the volume for that period of time as illustrated in Figure 2-6. A vertical scale can be used along the bottom of the chart to help plot the data.

The significance of rising and declining volume relative to various price movements will be discussed in detail throughout this course.

Open Interest

Open interest represents the total number of outstanding contracts for a particular commodity or futures contract. It is not applicable to stocks. Open interest is frequently plotted as a solid line along the bottom of the bar chart, usually just above the volume.

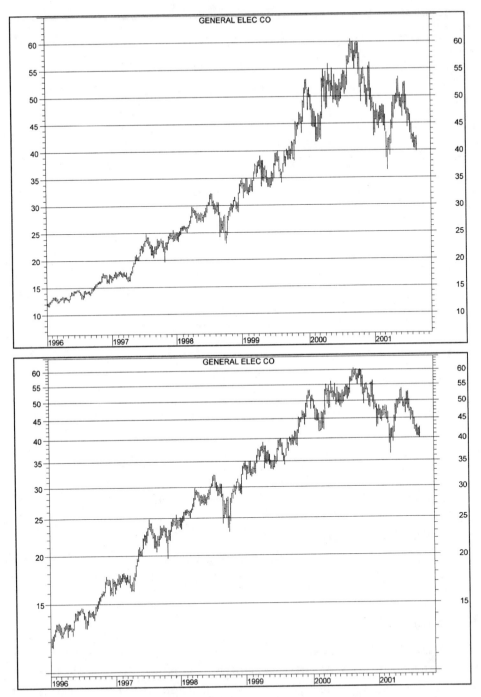

Figure 2-5 Comparison of Arithmetic (*top*) and Logarithmic (*bottom*) Scales

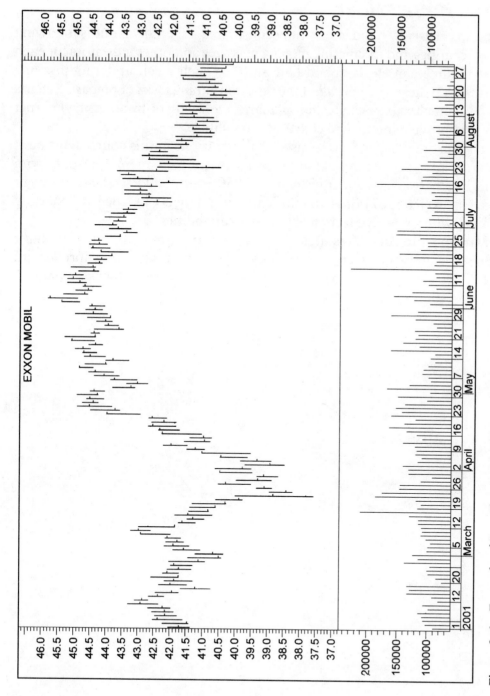

Figure 2-6   Example of Bar Chart with Volume Activity Plotted along the Bottom

Chart Preparation

Preparing charts by hand is very time-consuming, especially if one is following many securities and calculating moving averages and other indicators for each security. One can easily spend half an hour each week updating just one chart. Fortunately, virtually all of the time-consuming tasks of preparing charts can be eliminated by using technical analysis software or by accessing Internet sites that provide interactive charting capabilities.

The vast majority of charts used as illustrations in this course have been prepared using the technical analysis software package *MetaStock* from Equis International (www.equis.com or 3950 South 700 East, Suite 100, Salt Lake City, UT 84107). It is an excellent and relatively inexpensive charting package with extensive technical analysis capabilities.

Various Internet sites (such as www.bigcharts.com) already have impressive interactive technical analysis features that will only improve with time. They are another practical alternative to preparing charts by hand.

True or False Quiz

Circle T if the statement is true or F if the statement is false.

T   F   1. A bar chart for a stock plots only its closing price and volume for each time period.

T   F   2. Monthly bar charts are frequently used to determine the short-term trend of stock prices.

T   F   3. On a bar chart, the horizontal tic to the right of the vertical bar (connecting high and low prices) represents the closing price for the period.

T   F   4. A weekly bar chart is a condensed version of a daily chart when the same price data is used.

T   F   5. When the vertical scale on a bar chart is logarithmic, the distances between 10 to 20 and 20 to 30 are equal.

T   F   6. Technical analysis software packages can be used to calculate and plot a variety of basic and advanced technical indicators quickly.

Answers

1. *False.* A bar chart for a stock plots high, low, and closing prices for each time period. In addition, volume is typically plotted at the bottom of the bar chart.
2. *False.* Monthly bar charts are normally used to gain a long-term perspective. Hourly or daily bar charts are often used to determine the short-term trend of stock prices.
3. *True.* See Figure 2-2.
4. *True.* See Figures 2-3 and 2-4 for an illustration.
5. *False.* On an arithmetic scale the distances between 10 to 20 and 20 to 30 are equal. On a logarithmic scale the distance between 20 to 30 is half as much as between 10 to 20 because it represents a 50 percent increase in price, while a 100 percent increases occurs from 10 to 20.
6. *True.*

PROFITABLE CHART PATTERNS

MAJOR REVERSAL CHART PATTERNS

Market prices move in trends of varying duration and definition. While the trend is changing, identifiable chart patterns frequently develop. These patterns, known as *reversal chart patterns,* help identify when the market is changing direction, either from up to down or down to up. The primary importance of reversal patterns is that they help one sell securities before considerable price declines and cover short sales ahead of considerable advances.

Technicians have discovered many reversal chart patterns. Some occur frequently; others are rarely seen. Some are very reliable; others don't result in the price movements one would expect. This lesson presents a select group of reversal chart patterns, ones that have proven to be of considerable validity over many years.

Before examining the characteristics of numerous reversal chart patterns, let's try to understand the forces behind a trend reversal. The forming of a market top and subsequent price reversal to the downside occurs as a result of supply overcoming demand (known as distribution). The opposite occurs at market bottoms when demand overcomes supply (known as accumulation). In both cases, this overcoming activity typically occurs gradually. Prices swing back and forth (in a manner that develops a reversal chart pattern) in a sideways fashion of some sort until a complete reversal is accomplished.

Keep in mind that the greater the time it takes for a reversal chart pattern to form, the more reliable the signal generated is, as well as the time horizon (short-, intermediate-, or long-term) forecasted by the signal. Over the years, technicians have found the following reversal chart patterns to be worth looking for:

1. Key reversals.
2. Head and shoulders tops and bottoms.
3. Rounding tops and bottoms (saucers).
4. Ascending and descending triangles.
5. Rectangles.
6. Double and triple tops and bottoms.
7. Diamond.
8. Rising and falling wedges.
9. V formations (spikes).

Let's examine each pattern in detail.

Key Reversals

Figure 3-1 illustrates a key reversal top. A key reversal bottom is shown in Figure 3-2.

Typical Price Action   Key reversals occur during one period (usually one day) of market activity. A key reversal top is the result of prices quickly moving higher (to a new high in an uptrend) than the previous period's high, but closing near the lows of the day (and, at times, even lower than the previous period's low). Key reversal tops appear regularly in thinly traded stocks after an active advance.

The opposite occurs for a key reversal bottom. Prices first move sharply lower (to a new low in a downtrend) than the previous period's low and then move to the upside closing near the high for the day (and often higher than the previous period's high). A key reversal bottom is frequently called a *selling climax* as it often occurs at the end of a panic decline.

Typical Volume Action   Key reversals normally are accompanied by unusually high volume.

Frequency of Occurrence   Key reversals appear often. They can develop in and of themselves or as a part of a larger chart pattern (such as the top of the head in a head and shoulders top formation).

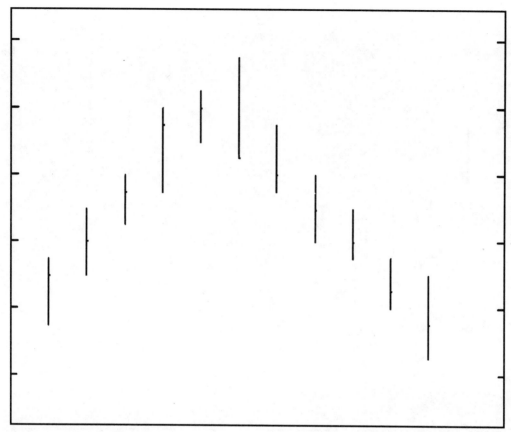

Figure 3-1   Key Reversal Top

Technical Significance   A key reversal has only short-term (minor trend) significance. Its significance is, however, greatly enhanced if one or more of the following occurs:

1. The period's high penetrates the previous period's high significantly for a key reversal top or the period's low penetrates the previous period's low significantly for a key reversal bottom.
2. The key reversal period was preceded by a long, unbroken trend.
3. The period's closing price was below (for a key reversal top) or above (for a key reversal bottom) one or more immediately prior period ranges.
4. The period volume was particularly high.

29

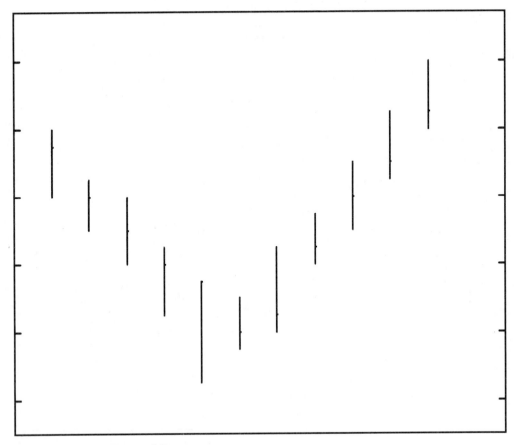

Figure 3-2   Key Reversal Bottom

Head and Shoulders Tops and Bottoms

A head and shoulders top is illustrated in Figure 3-3. Figure 3-4 shows a head and shoulders bottom.

Typical Price Action   The head and shoulders top formation is one of the most common and most reliable chart patterns. It consists of a left shoulder, head, and right shoulder as shown in Figure 3-3. The left shoulder is typically formed at the end of an extensive advance. After prices drop from the peak of the left shoulder, they rally to a new high and then decline to near the low of the left shoulder to form the head part of the head and shoulders chart pattern. A final advance to a peak lower than that of the head followed by a decline in prices forms the right shoulder and completes the chart pattern.

A neckline can be drawn across the bottom of the left shoulder, head, and right shoulder. When the neckline is broken, you receive confirmation of a reversal in the trend. After moving lower, it is not uncommon for prices to pull back to the neckline before continuing their descent.

Head and shoulders bottoms are simply the inverse of head and shoulders tops. In some occasions, bottoms appear flatter than tops.

The majority of head and shoulder formations are not perfectly symmetrical. The neckline can be horizontal but often slopes up or down. However, for a head and shoulders top on an upsloping neckline, the lowest part of the right shoulder should be appreciably lower than the top of the left shoulder. The inverse is true for head and shoulder bottoms.

Figure 3-3   Head and Shoulders Top

Figure 3-4   Head and Shoulders Bottom

Typical Volume Action   For a head and shoulders top, volume is heavy on the rally portion of the left shoulder. Volume declines on the dip from the left shoulder peak and then again is heavy on the rally up to the top of the head. A reduction in volume occurs on the decline from the top of the head. The ensuing rally to create the right shoulder occurs on less volume than on previous rallies in this formation.

For a head and shoulders bottom, volume picks up on each rally with greater volume on the rally completing the right shoulder than on the rally completing the head. Between rallies, volume diminishes. If the neckline is broken on relatively low volume, it could be indicating a false signal, and a retest of lows may be forthcoming.

Frequency of Occurrence   Head and shoulders chart patterns occur relatively frequently.

Technical Significance   The minimum price objective after a head and shoulders neckline break is the same distance from the top of the head to the neckline. (The move prior to the head and shoulders pattern must be at least as great as the distance from the top of the head to the neckline.)

Rounding Tops and Bottoms (Saucers)

Rounding tops and bottoms, also known as saucers, are illustrated in Figures 3-5 and 3-6, respectively.

Figure 3-5   Rounding Top

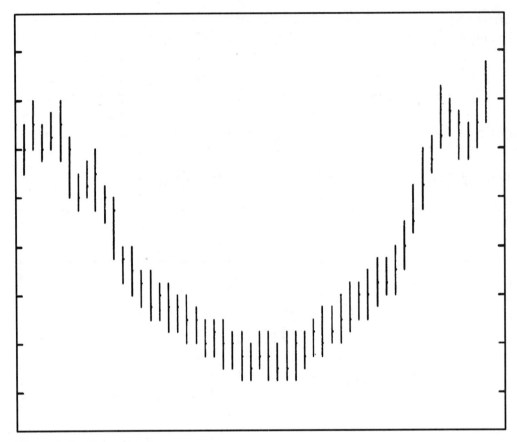

Figure 3-6   Rounding Bottom

Typical Price Action   Unlike many other reversal chart patterns, rounding tops and bottoms form as a result of a very gradual shift in supply and demand. A fairly symmetrical change in the direction of the trend occurs.

Typical Volume Action   Volume declines throughout the first portion of the pattern (up to the top for a rounding top or bottom for a rounding bottom) and then rises on the decline in prices from the top (rounding top) or rally from the bottom (rounding bottom).

Frequency of Occurrence   Rounding tops and bottoms are very rare, but do occur occasionally in interest sensitive and other securities where wide-swinging price fluctuations are unusual.

Technical Significance   The significance of the rounding top and bottom patterns is simply to identify that a reversal in the trend has occurred. It implies no measured amount of movement in the new direction of the trend.

Ascending and Descending Triangles

Ascending and descending triangle chart patterns are illustrated in Figures 3-7 and 3-8, respectively.

Typical Price Action   For an ascending triangle, prices swing between a horizontal top boundary line and an upward sloping bottom boundary line. An ascending triangle develops when demand is growing, but continues to

Figure 3-7   Ascending Triangle

Figure 3-8   Descending Triangle

meet supply at a certain price level. Once the supply is absorbed, prices break out of the pattern and move up rapidly.

For a descending triangle, the opposite is true. Prices swing between a downward sloping top boundary line and a horizontal bottom boundary line. A descending triangle is formed when supply is growing, but continues to meet demand at a certain price level. Once the demand is exhausted, prices break out of the pattern and quickly move lower. Triangles are considered intermediate-term patterns, usually taking from one to three months to complete.

Typical Volume Action   Volume decreases as prices move toward the apex of either the ascending or descending triangle. Breakouts are accompanied by a marked increase in trading volume.

Frequency of Occurrence　Both ascending and descending triangles appear regularly on daily charts. They are less frequent, but still not unusual, on weekly charts.

Technical Significance　Ascending and descending triangles offer excellent profit opportunities. The ascending triangle provides a bullish outlook, while the descending triangle suggests a bearish future.

Both types of triangles have similar measuring implications in regard to how far to expect prices to move after the breakout. Let's examine the measuring implication for an ascending triangle. It is illustrated in Figure 3-7.

First, a line is drawn parallel to the bottom boundary from the top of the first rally that initiated the pattern. This line will slope up and to the right. Prices will ordinarily move up until they reach this line.

The same measuring principle in inverse applies to descending triangles.

Rectangles

Examples of bullish and bearish rectangle chart patterns are provided in Figures 3-9 and 3-10, respectively.

Typical Price Action　A rectangle pattern consists of sideways price movements that are contained within two horizontal (or near horizontal) lines at the top and the bottom. This area is also known as a *trading area* or *range*. Rectangles are formed when there is consistent supply of a security at a certain price and demand at a certain lower price. When the price reaches the lower price, the security is purchased, driving up the price until such time as it reaches the upper boundary and people are ready to sell and drive the price back to the lower boundary. This occurs repeatedly until one side or the other gives way and the pattern is broken.

A closing price outside the upper or lower boundary line implies the direction of the trend. If the closing price is above the upper boundary line, the probability is that prices will move higher. On the other hand, if the closing price is below the lower boundary line, prices will likely fall.

Typical Volume Action　Volume action can give a clue as to whether the rectangle formation will ultimately be broken to the upside or downside. If volume is relatively higher on upward price swings than moves to the

Figure 3-9   Bullish Rectangle

downside, it is likely the breakout will occur on the upside. On the other hand, if volume is relatively higher on downward price swings than moves to the upside, it is likely there will be a downside breakout of the rectangle.

Frequency of Occurrence   Rectangles occur regularly and are easy to spot.

Technical Significance   A close above the upper boundary line or below the lower boundary line signals the direction of the trend. No measurement guidelines are established by rectangles for the distance prices will move in the direction of a breakout.

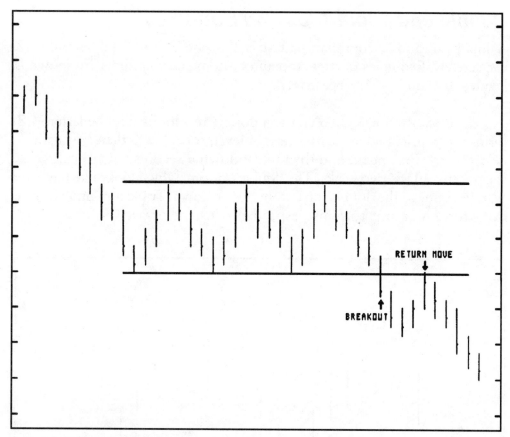

Figure 3-10   Bearish Rectangle

TECHNICAL ANALYSIS TIP

Some short-term traders make trades within well defined rectangles. They buy when prices reach the bottom boundary and sell short when prices reach the upper boundary. To protect themselves in the event of a pattern breakout, each time they buy or sell short, they also place stop-loss orders just outside the lower or upper boundary lines to minimize any potential losses. If the pattern is broken, they are stopped-out at a small loss, and they quickly place a new order in the direction of the breakout.

Double and Triple Tops and Bottoms

A double top and bottom chart pattern is illustrated in Figures 3-11 and 3-12, respectively. Examples of triple top and bottom chart patterns are shown in Figures 3-13 and 3-14, respectively.

Typical Price Action   On a chart, a double top looks like the letter **M**. It forms when prices advance to a certain level, turn down, then rise again to near the previous peak, and then move down a second time to below the valley between the two peaks. The double bottom, which looks like the letter **W**, is the same as the double top except upside down. Triple tops and bottoms make three tops and bottoms, respectively, instead of two.

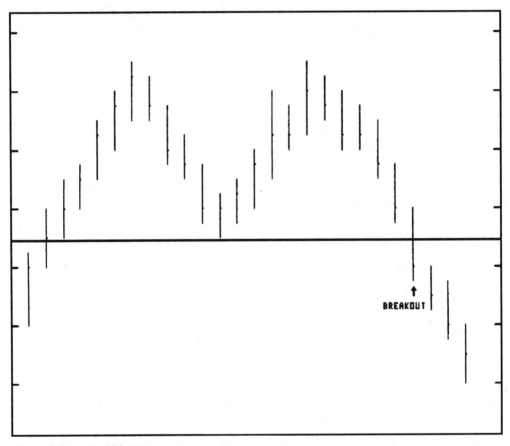

BREAKOUT

Figure 3-11   Double Top

Figure 3-12 Double Bottom

Typical Volume Action For a double top, volume on the rise to the second peak is less than on the first peak. If volume is relatively higher, chances of a double top occurring are reduced. For a double bottom, volume shows a marked increase on the rally from the second bottom.

For triple tops, volume is relatively less on the second advance than the first and even less on the third advance. For triple bottoms, volume is relatively higher on the second rally than the first and still greater on the third advance.

Frequency of Occurrence True double tops and bottoms are rare; triple tops and bottoms are even rarer.

Technical Significance Double tops and bottoms are popular chart patterns, but are frequently mislabeled. In any uptrend, after a reaction, each new wave up will appear to be making a double top. However, the vast majority of the time, prices carry to new highs and no double top is formed. One must wait for confirmation of the pattern, which does not occur until the price goes below the low price of the valley between the two peaks (or above the high price of the peak between two valleys for double bottoms).

A further test of validity is the time element. Peaks should be separated by a significant reaction. If the two tops (peaks) are near, they could very well be part of a consolidation area. As a yardstick, use the criteria of peaks being one month apart and the valley being at least 15 percent lower than the top peak price.

Figure 3-13   Triple Top

Figure 3-14   Triple Bottom

True double and triple tops and bottoms do have measuring implications. Expect prices to move in the direction of the reversal at least the distance from the valley to the peak.

Diamond

The diamond formation derives its names from its pictorial resemblance on a chart to the diamond figure as illustrated in Figure 3-15.

Typical Price Action   The diamond formation is actually the combination of two other chart patterns, namely the expanding triangle and the symmetrical triangle. During the expanding triangle part, price swings widen.

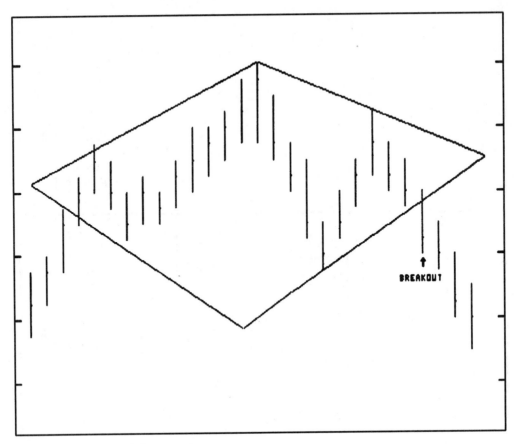

Figure 3-15   Diamond Formation

Subsequently, price swings narrow during the symmetrical triangle part of the diamond formation. The formation is completed when one of the boundary lines forming the symmetrical triangle part of the diamond formation is broken.

The diamond formation can also occur in a fashion similar to a complex head and shoulders pattern with a V-shaped neckline. Although the diamond formation can turn out to be a continuation pattern, it usually is a reversal pattern.

Typical Volume Action   Volume increases during the first half of the diamond formation (the part that looks like an expanding triangle) and declines gradually during the second half (the part that looks like a symmetrical triangle). Volume typically increases on the breakout from the diamond formation.

Frequency of Occurrence   The diamond formation is seen rarely. It normally appears at market tops and not at market bottoms, since it requires a relatively active (high volume) environment to develop.

Technical Significance   On a breakout of the diamond formation, prices should move a minimum amount equal to the distance from the top to the bottom of the pattern. Generally, prices move farther than the minimum measurement.

Rising and Falling Wedges

Figures 3-16 and 3-17 illustrate rising and falling wedge chart patterns, respectively.

BREAKOUT

Figure 3-16   Rising Wedge

Figure 3-17   Falling Wedge

Typical Price Action   Wedges are characterized by prices fluctuating between two converging boundary lines. For a rising wedge, the boundary lines are slanted upward with the lower line being at a steeper angle than the upper line. For a falling wedge, the boundary lines are slanted down and the upper line is at a steeper angle than the lower line. Breakouts normally occur at least two-thirds of the way to the apex of the converging boundary lines.

On a daily chart, a wedge formation typically takes three or more weeks to complete.

Typical Volume Action   Trading volume in a wedge gradually diminishes as prices move toward the apex of the wedge and then rises on the breakout.

Frequency of Occurrence   Wedges are formed on a regular basis.

Technical Significance   The rising wedge implies a situation that is growing weaker from a technical perspective. When prices break through the lower line of a rising wedge, they usually fall in earnest. Sell signals generated by breakouts below the lower line of rising wedges are more reliable in bear markets than in bull markets.

The falling wedge typifies a situation that is getting stronger from a technical perspective. When prices break through the upper boundary of a falling wedge, they tend to move sideways for a period of time before beginning to rise.

V Formations (Spikes)

Contrary to most reversal patterns which gradually change direction, the V formation (otherwise known as a spike) suddenly reverses the trend with little warning. Examples of a V formation top and bottom are provided in Figures 3-18 and 3-19, respectively.

Typical Price Action   Prices move quickly either up or down and move beyond expectations. Prices become overextended and snap back quickly without warning.

Typical Volume Action   Volume is relatively heavy throughout the pattern.

Frequency of Occurrence   V formations develop regularly, particularly in volatile, popular stocks.

Technical Significance   V formations occur so quickly and with such little warning that the pattern can be spotted only after the fact and only after a significant move in the opposite direction has already occurred. Thus, profit opportunities are limited with regard to V formation chart patterns.

Figure 3-18   V Top

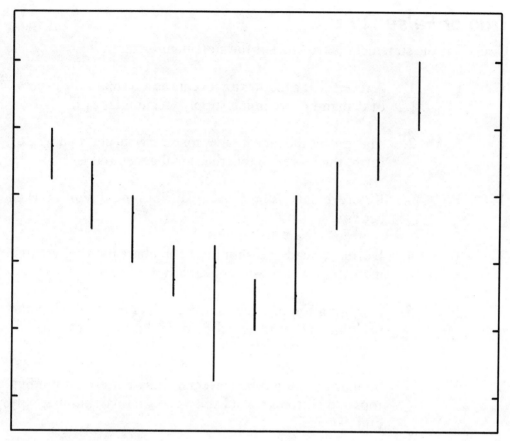

Figure 3-19   V Bottom

True or False Quiz

Circle T if the statement is true or F if the statement is false.

T   F   1. A reversal at a market top occurs as a result of the process of demand overcoming supply (accumulation).

T   F   2. The greater the time it takes for a reversal chart pattern to form, the more reliable the signal generated is.

T   F   3. Key reversals usually occur during one day of market activity.

T   F   4. During a head and shoulders top chart pattern, volume increases on each successive rally.

T   F   5. Confirmation of a reversal in trend is received when the neckline of a head and shoulders chart top or bottom is broken.

T   F   6. Similar to many other reversal chart patterns, rounding tops and bottoms result from a very gradual shift in supply and demand.

T   F   7. Ascending and descending triangles occur with such little warning that you can spot the patterns only after the fact. Profit opportunities are limited with regard to ascending and descending triangles.

T   F   8. A double top looks like the letter **M**.

T   F   9. The diamond formation is seen frequently at market bottoms.

T   F   10. Wedge chart patterns form when prices fluctuate between two converging boundary lines.

T   F   11. The chart below shows a rounding top chart pattern.

T   F   12. When prices break through the neckline of the head and shoulders bottom pattern shown in the following chart, it is likely that they will rise to at least $13.75.

T   F   13. The chart below illustrates a bullish rectangle formation.

T   F   14. The rally from point A in the following chart would likely occur on expanding volume.

Answers

1. *False.* Demand overcomes supply (accumulation) forming market bottoms. A reversal at a market top occurs when supply overcomes demand (distribution).
2. *True.*
3. *True.*
4. *False.* For a head and shoulders top, volume is heavy on the rally portion of the left shoulder. Volume is again heavy on the rally to the top of the head. However, the final rally to create the right shoulder occurs on less volume than on previous rallies in this formation.
5. *True.*
6. *False.* Rounding tops and bottoms are unlike many other reversal chart patterns that form from a much quicker shift in supply and demand.
7. *False.* Ascending and descending triangles offer excellent profit opportunities. They are relatively easy to spot as they develop and have measuring implications in regard to how far prices are expected to move after a breakout.
8. *True.*
9. *False.* The diamond formation is seen rarely. It normally appears at market tops, not market bottoms.
10. *True.*
11. *False.* The chart reflects a key reversal top. See Figure 3-5 for an illustration of a rounding top.
12. *True.* It is probable that prices will move a distance away from the neckline equal to that from the top of the head to the neckline.
13. *True.*
14. *True.* Refer to the section on the double bottom chart pattern.

CONSOLIDATION FORMATIONS

Consolidation formations occur when security prices move up or down too fast and reach a level at which the demand or supply that produced the move is completely absorbed. At that point three things can occur. First, prices can reverse their trend, in which case you would likely see a reversal pattern develop. Second, prices can decline or rise to a support level before building up steam again. Third, prices can move sideways, creating a consolidation formation from which to base a further move in the direction of the trend.

In essence a consolidation formation can be defined as a sideways price movement that temporarily interrupts an up or down move in prices. There are many consolidation formations. This lesson will teach four of the most reliable ones, namely flags, pennants, head and shoulders continuation patterns, and symmetrical triangles.

Flags

A flag pattern in an uptrend is illustrated in Figure 4-1.

Typical Price Action   A flag pattern, as one would expect, looks like a flag on a chart. It represents a pause in a quick, almost vertical, up or down move in prices. Prices move sideways forming a flag-like pattern, break out from that pattern, and then continue in the same direction as before.

Typical Volume Action   Volume is extremely heavy before the flag formation begins. As the pattern develops, volume diminishes to a relatively low level. Finally, volume explodes as prices complete and break out of the flag pattern.

Figure 4-1 Flag

Frequency of Occurrence Flags appear regularly on daily charts, but because of the short time they take to develop (typically less than four weeks), they are rarely seen on weekly charts and are nonexistent on monthly charts.

Technical Significance Flags typically appear at the halfway point of an up or down move. Therefore, one can expect prices to move about the same distance after the breakout from the flag pattern as they did just prior to the pattern.

Pennants

Figure 4-2 illustrates a pennant chart pattern that occurs in an uptrend.

Typical Price Action   Pennants and flags have the same characteristics except that a pennant is formed by converging, rather than parallel, boundary lines. Pennants slant down in uptrends and up in downtrends. As with flags, pennant consolidations are characteristic of fast up and down moves in prices.

Figure 4-2   Pennant

Typical Volume Action   Volume is extremely heavy before the pennant formation begins. As the pattern develops, volume diminishes to a relatively low level. Finally, volume increases significantly as prices complete and break out of the pennant pattern.

Frequency of Occurrence   Pennants should take less than four weeks to complete and break out. Therefore, like flags, they are more identifiable in daily charts than weekly charts and never appear on monthly charts. They occur most frequently in the last phase of bull markets and in the second stage of bear markets.

Technical Significance   Pennants typically appear about midway through an up or down move. Therefore, expect prices to move about the same distance after the breakout from the pennant pattern as they did just prior to the pattern.

Head and Shoulders Continuation Patterns

Bullish and bearish head and shoulders continuation patterns are illustrated in Figures 4-3 and 4-4, respectively.

Typical Price Action   Head and shoulders continuation patterns are inverted relative to the direction of the price trend before their appearance. When prices are trending lower, a head and shoulders continuation pattern appears similar to a head and shoulders top. (Refer to Lesson 3 for a complete description of head and shoulders tops and bottoms.) In an uptrend, a head and shoulders continuation pattern appears like a head and shoulders bottom.

Typical Volume Action   For the head and shoulders continuation pattern, volume decreases instead of increasing (as with the head and shoulders top) on the left shoulder and head, as well as the right shoulder. Volume does resemble that of head and shoulders tops and bottoms on breakout from the continuation patterns; it is relatively heavy.

Frequency of Occurrence   Head and shoulders continuation patterns occur occasionally.

Figure 4-3 Bullish Head and Shoulders Continuation Pattern

Technical Significance   The measurement characteristics that apply to head and shoulders tops and bottoms sometimes work with head and shoulders continuation patterns, but not with enough regularity to warrant reliance on them. Technical significance is limited to notation that prices are continuing an uptrend or downtrend upon a breakout from the head and shoulders continuation pattern.

Symmetrical Triangle

An illustration of a symmetrical triangle formation in an uptrend is provided in Figure 4-5.

Figure 4-4   Bearish Head and Shoulders Continuation Pattern

Typical Price Action   Prices swing in a narrowing fashion between downslanting upper and upslanting lower boundary lines that are fairly symmetrical in nature. There must be a minimum of four reversal points in the triangle. A breakout can occur at any time between two-thirds of the way to the apex and the apex.

Typical Volume Action   Volume diminishes as prices approach the apex of the triangle. On a valid upside breakout, volume is heavy; on a valid downside breakout, volume is often light at first and then picks up significantly after a few days.

Beware of upside breakouts on light volume and downside break-outs accompanied by heavy volume. They could be a warning of false moves.

Frequency of Occurrence   Symmetrical triangles appear regularly on price charts.

Technical Significance   On a valid upside breakout, you can expect prices to continue upward until they reach a line drawn parallel to the lower boundary line. The opposite is true for a valid downside breakout.

Figure 4-5   Symmetrical Triangle

True or False Quiz

Circle T if the statement is true or F if the statement is false.

T   F   1. A consolidation formation can be defined as a sideways price movement that temporarily interrupts an up or down move in prices.

T   F   2. After a consolidation formation, prices move in the opposite direction than before the consolidation formation.

T   F   3. Many of the characteristics of flag and pennant chart patterns are the same.

T   F   4. A flag is formed by converging boundary lines.

T   F   5. Head and shoulders continuation patterns are inverted relative to the direction of the price trend prior to their appearance.

T   F   6. On a valid upside breakout of a symmetrical triangle pattern, volume is relatively light.

Answers

1. *True.*
2. *False.* A consolidation formation "temporarily interrupts" an up or down move in prices. Prices continue in the same direction upon a breakout from a consolidation formation.
3. *True.*
4. *False.* A flag is formed by parallel boundary lines as illustrated in Figure 4-1. A pennant is formed by converging boundary lines as illustrated in Figure 4-2.
5. *True.*
6. *False.* Volume is relatively heavy on a valid upside breakout of a symmetrical triangle pattern.

GAPS

In addition to reversal and consolidation formations, a group of chart patterns based on gaps in price activity appear on charts.

A *gap* represents a price range on a chart at which no trading takes place (no securities trade hands). Gaps can appear in an uptrend (as shown in Figure 5-1) signifying market strength or a downtrend (as shown in Figure 5-2) suggesting market weakness. When a gap occurs in an uptrend, the current period's low is higher than the previous period's high. In a downtrend, a gap appears when the current period's high is lower than the previous period's low.

Frequency of Appearance

Gaps occur more frequently on charts covering short time frames (such as hourly or daily) than they do on longer term charts (such as those plotting weekly or monthly data). However, they are of greater significance on long-term charts than short-term charts. The reason for that is easily explained.

Gaps are common on daily charts because they can be created on a daily basis (20 or more times during a month). At the end of each day, an opportunity exists that the current day's high (or low) price will be lower than (or higher than) any price at which that stock trades on the next day. However, on a monthly chart, only one opportunity each month exists for a gap to occur. It is rare, and thus of great significance, that the high (or low) price for the current month will not be crossed at some time during the next month and create a gap. About the only time gaps occur on monthly charts is when a panic rise or decline occurs at the end of the month.

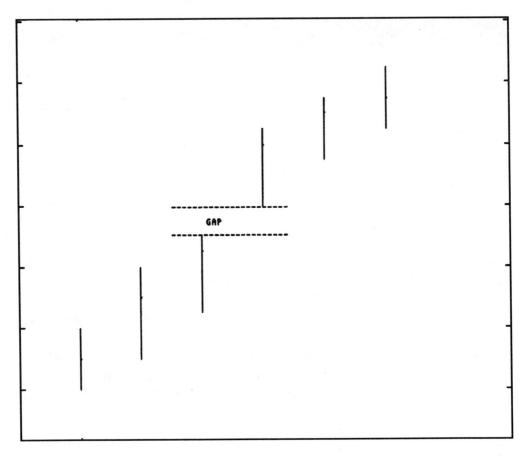

Figure 5-1   Gap in an Uptrend

Insignificant Gaps

Some gaps are significant while others are meaningless. Gaps that are not significant include:

1. A gap caused by a stock trading an amount equal to the minimum permitted change in price.
2. For higher-priced stocks, the spread between successive bids is frequently $0.10 to $0.50. Gaps equal to the normal interval between successive bids are of no technical significance.
3. For medium- to high-priced issues that have low trading volume, gaps are regular and numerous. They are also not significant.

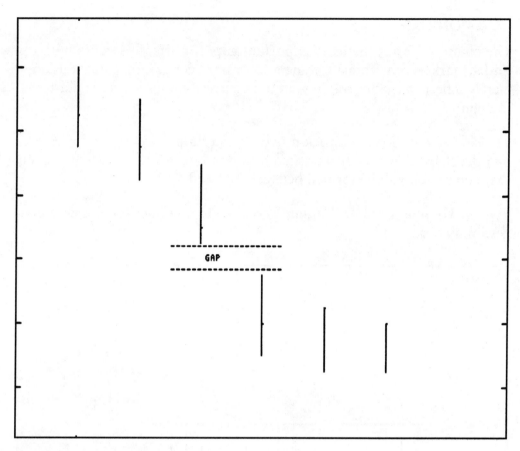

Figure 5-2 Gap in a Downtrend

4. Ex-dividend gaps frequently occur when a company pays a dividend. They are actually an alteration to the book value of an issue and have no trend implications.

Significant Gaps

Four types of gaps regularly occur on charts. One type (common) is of less significance than the other three types (breakaway, runaway, and exhaustion). An example and discussion highlighting the characteristics of each type of gap follows.

COMMON GAP

The common gap is the least important gap. It normally occurs in thinly traded markets or within a trading area or price congestion pattern. It often merely reflects a lack of trading interest. Three common gaps are illustrated in Figure 5-3.

Typical Price Action   A stock moves in a certain price range, say $15 to $25 per share. A gap is then created by a jump from $22 to $25. It is likely that congestion will be formed between $22 and $25.

Typical Volume Action   Volume is relatively low due to being in a congestion pattern.

Figure 5-3   Common Gaps

Frequency of Occurrence   Common gaps occur often as the name "common" suggests.

Technical Significance   Common gaps are of little forecasting significance. However, they can alert technicians to a congestion pattern that is in the process of being constructed.

BREAKAWAY GAP

Most breakouts from a horizontal price boundary are attended by a breakaway gap. An example is provided in Figure 5-4.

Typical Price Action   A breakaway gap occurs on a price breakout through a horizontal pattern boundary. Typically, the horizontal pattern boundary is part of a price congestion pattern (such as an ascending triangle) and the breakout marks its completion. For example, suppose a stock has traded up to $21 per share, stopped, and turned lower over and over. This would suggest both a persistent demand for and a large supply of stock available for sale at the $21 level. Current stock holders observe the price action and make their stock available at the $21 level or figure that once the stock breaks the $21 barrier, it will go much higher. (Therefore, they hold their stock for the time being.) This creates a vacuum so that once the supply of stock at $21 is absorbed, the next buyer finds none available at $21.01 to $21.49. He or she must bid $21.50 and thus create a breakaway gap.

Typical Volume Action   Volume is normally heavy when a breakaway gap occurs. If volume is higher before the gap than after, chances are about 50–50 that the gap will be filled on the next minor reaction. If volume is higher after the gap than before, chances are slim that near-term reactions will fill the gap.

TECHNICAL ANALYSIS TIP

Almost every legitimate breakout from a price congestion formation is accompanied by a breakaway gap. Although not all breakaway gaps appear on charts (because they occur during the day and not between one day's closing price and the following day's opening price), beware of breakouts not accompanied by gaps. Gaps seldom occur in false breakouts (those which do not follow through in the direction of the breakout).

Frequency of Occurrence   Breakaway gaps appear much less frequently than common gaps, but often enough to warrant watching for them.

Technical Significance   Breakaway gaps are highly significant. They often signal the start of a rapid price move in the direction of the breakout. In the case of an upward move, this is due to buying demand that is stronger

Figure 5-4   Breakaway Gap

than selling pressure, often resulting in prices moving up quickly until balance is restored between supply and demand. The opposite is true for down movements.

RUNAWAY GAP

The runaway gap is a reliable indicator of a strong underlying trend. It is sometimes called a *continuation* or *measuring gap.* An example of a runaway gap is provided in Figure 5-5.

Typical Price Action   Runaway gaps occur in the middle of fast up or down price movements. This is typically when price quotes are moving rapidly and easily relative to the volume of transactions.

Typical Volume Action   Runaway gaps typically occur on moderate volume when the price is seemingly moving effortlessly. At times, runaway gaps are accompanied by relatively high volume, which increases the probability of a strong underlying trend in the direction of the move.

TECHNICAL ANALYSIS TIP

Runaway gaps frequently occur about halfway through an up or down price move. Therefore, you can expect that prices will move about the same percentage amount from the gap to the end of the move (a congestion or reversal pattern) as it has from the beginning of the move to the gap. Since it is the same "percentage" move, the vertical distance on a chart is about equal on a logarithmic scaled chart. On a chart with an arithmetic vertical scale, the advance will be greater (after the gap) than the vertical distance (before the gap) on a chart; declines will be less.

Frequency of Occurrence   Runaway gaps occur less often than common or breakaway gaps but are more significant from a technical perspective.

Technical Significance   Runaway gaps are a sign of significant strength in an uptrend or weakness in a downtrend. They are easy to distinguish from common or breakaway gaps. Distinguishing a runaway gap from

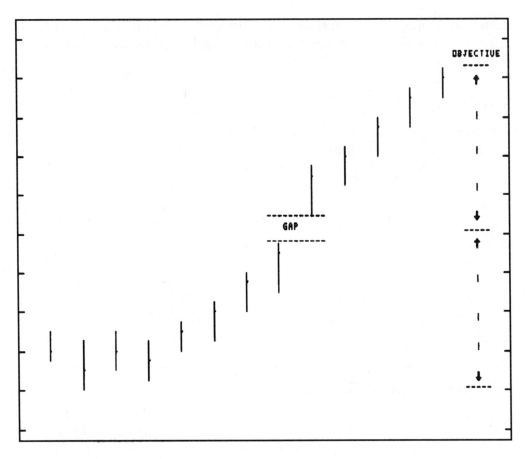

Figure 5-5   Runaway Gap

an exhaustion **gap** is not easy initially. However, the price and volume action on the day after the gap provides the evidence you need for a correct interpretation.

Runaway gaps usually are not filled until the next intermediate or major price move. This typically occurs only after a considerable amount of time has passed.

Multiple runaway gaps can occur. When two or more such gaps occur, the measuring implications are less certain. One should act conservatively in these situations, recognizing that each additional runaway gap brings nearer a price top or bottom.

EXHAUSTION GAP

An exhaustion gap is the last gasp of an up or down price move. It is very difficult to distinguish from a runaway gap until after the fact. An exhaustion gap is illustrated in Figure 5-6.

Typical Price Movement   An exhaustion gap is associated with a quick up or down movement in price (like a runaway gap). Prices move rapidly until, suddenly, they meet an abundance of supply in an up move or demand in a down move. At that point, the move is ended abruptly by a day of very high trading volume. It is not uncommon for an exhaustion gap to appear between the next to the last and the last day of a move.

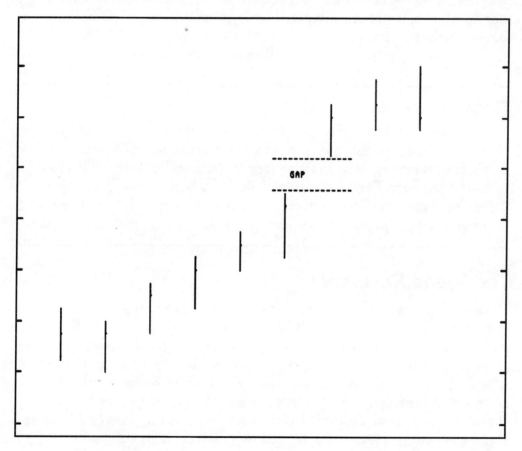

Figure 5-6   Exhaustion Gap

Typical Volume Activity   An exhaustion gap is usually accompanied by a day of very high volume on a relative basis.

Frequency of Occurrence   By their nature, exhaustion gaps occur with low frequency at the end of up or down price moves.

Technical Significance   An exhaustion gap implies the end of an up or down move. After an exhaustion gap, you can expect an area pattern to form that eventually leads to price continuation or reversal. Even if price does eventually continue in the direction it was moving prior to the exhaustion gap, antici- pate a time delay in the price advance or decline (which may warrant closing out your positions, depending on your investment time horizon). On the day following a gap, if a reversal day develops with the closing prices back to near the edge of the gap, it is extremely probable that the gap is an exhaustion rather than a runaway gap. Exhaustion gaps are normally filled in two to five days.

TECHNICAL ANALYSIS TIP

Exhaustion and runaway gaps have similar characteristics that make them difficult to distinguish from each other initially. When one of these gaps occurs, immediately place protective stop-loss orders close to the gap price. Even if you think it will be an exhaustion gap, you do not need to immediately sell your positions (or cover short positions) or reverse your positions. You can wait until more evidence is present.

The Island Reversal

Occasionally, a section of a chart is isolated from the rest of the chart by gaps appearing at approximately the same horizontal price level. When this pattern occurs, it is known as an *island reversal*. Typically, the gap leading to the island reversal is an exhaustion gap, and the gap completing the island reversal pattern is a breakaway gap as illustrated in Figure 5-7.

An island reversal can represent one or more periods of trading activity. It can also be part of another chart pattern (such as the head of a head and shoulders pattern). It is characterized by relatively high volume.

By itself, an island reversal does not suggest that a long-term top or bottom has occurred. However, prices do frequently retrace the minor move that

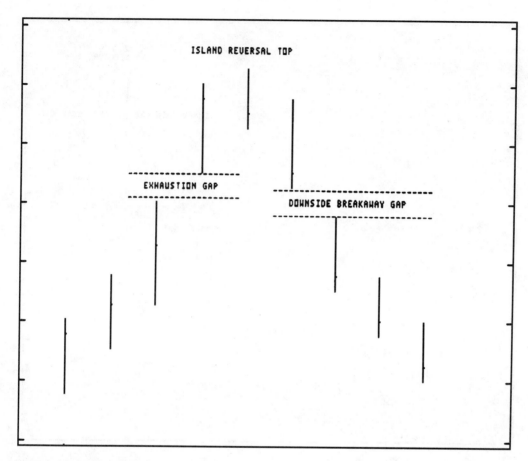

Figure 5-7   Island Reversal

preceded it. Much of that retracement is accomplished by the time an island reversal is charted, thereby minimizing the value of any trading opportunity.

The Total Picture

Figure 5-8 illustrates a progression of gap occurrences (excluding common gaps which could occur throughout). An upward breakaway gap typically releases prices from a congestion pattern. A runaway gap increases the upward momentum. An exhaustion gap signals an approaching top that could be an island reversal. Finally, a downside breakaway gap starts things in the opposite direction.

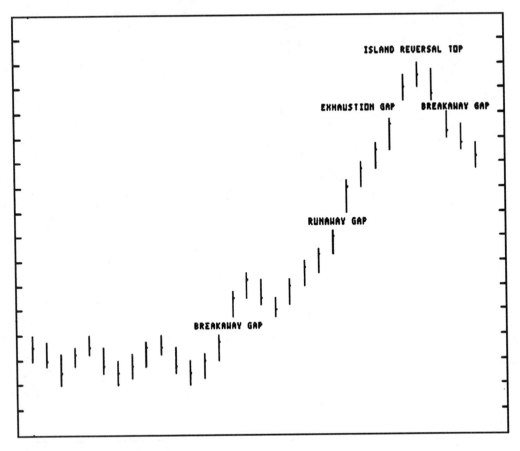

Figure 5-8   Progression of Gaps

Typically, the gaps would not appear in as orderly a fashion as illustrated in Figure 5-8. Gaps could appear in any combination of order. For example, you could have multiple breakaway gaps and no runaway gaps in a particular up movement. Nonetheless, the significance of each type of gap remains as summarized in the following table:

Type of Gap	Significance	Signals
Common	Little	—
Breakaway	Great	Significant market move
Runaway	Great	Halfway point of a price movement
Exhaustion	Great	Very bearish or very bullish

A Wall Street Myth—Gaps Must Be Closed

When a gap occurs on a price chart, it is not uncommon to read or hear someone say that the price must come back and fill the gap that was created. Over time, the probability is that the gap will be filled, since most securities trade in certain price ranges. However, there is absolutely no reason why it *must* be closed. And, frequently, when it is closed, it is only after the price has moved far away from the gap.

For example, over a period of time, a stock moves in a range from $9 to $15 per share. One day it closes at the top of the range. The next day it opens at $15.50 and continues to move up from there, causing a gap to occur. The price subsequently climbs to $25 before retreating back through $15, closing the gap. The gap is closed, but only after a period of time (which could be months or years) has passed. Basing an investment decision on "gaps must be closed" is not sound investing.

True or False Quiz

Circle **T** if the statement is true or **F** if the statement is false.

T   F   1. Gaps in an uptrend signify market weakness.

T   F   2. Gaps occur more frequently on monthly charts than on daily charts.

T   F   3. Gaps appearing on weekly charts are more significant than those on daily charts.

T   F   4. Ex-dividend gaps have bearish trend implications.

T   F   5. The four types of gaps that regularly occur on charts are called common, breakaway, runaway, and exhaustion.

T   F   6. A common gap often occurs on a breakout from a price congestion area on a chart.

T   F   7. Runaway gaps are not immediately distinguishable from exhaustion gaps.

T   F   8. A breakaway gap frequently occurs about halfway through an up or down price move.

T   F   9. By itself, an island reversal signals a major top or bottom has occurred.

T   F   10. Gaps are always closed.

Refer to the following chart to answer questions 11 to 14.

T   F   11. The gap labeled A on the chart is a common gap.

T   F   12. The gap labeled A on the chart usually occurs on relatively heavy volume.

T   F   13. The gap labeled B on the chart is a runaway gap.

T   F   14. The gap labeled C on the chart is an exhaustion gap that is of little technical significance.

Answers

1. *False*. Gaps in an uptrend signify market strength.
2. *False*. Gaps appear more often on shorter-term daily charts than on longer-term monthly charts, since they have 20 or more times as many opportunities per month to form.
3. *True*. The longer the period of time covered by each bar on a bar chart, the more significant gaps become. Therefore, a gap on a weekly chart is of greater technical significance than a gap on a daily chart.
4. *False*. Ex-dividend gaps have no trend implications.
5. *True*.
6. *False*. A breakaway gap often occurs on a breakout from a price congestion area on a price chart. Common gaps normally appear within a trading area or price congestion pattern.
7. *True*. You must analyze price and volume action on the day(s) following the gap to determine whether it is a runaway or exhaustion gap.
8. *False*. A runaway gap, not a breakaway gap, frequently occurs about halfway through an up or down price move.
9. *False*. An island reversal signals a major top or bottom only when it is part of another reversal pattern, such as a head and shoulders top or bottom.
10. *False*. Most gaps are closed over time, but not all.
11. *False*. The gap labeled A on the chart is a breakaway gap.
12. *True*.
13. *True*.
14. *False*. The gap labeled C on the chart is an exhaustion gap. However, it is of great technical significance as it implies the end of an up price move.

KEY ANALYTICAL TOOLS

TRENDLINES AND CHANNELS

As shown in Lesson 1, one of the principles that technical analysis is based on is that prices move in trends. These trends can be up, down, or sideways as illustrated in Figure 6-1. An uptrend is characterized by successively higher highs and higher lows. A downtrend occurs on successively lower highs and lower lows. A sideways trend reflects horizontal price movement.

Trends can be brief or of long duration. They are typically classified as short-, intermediate-, or long-term. Although there are no generally accepted definitions of these three terms, short-term roughly refers to the next three months; intermediate-term is about three to six months from the present time; and long-term is considered to be approximately six months to one year from the current period.

Investors try to determine when prices are in an uptrend or downtrend. They profit by determining the trend and then following it until it is reversed. Of the many charting tools available, the trendline is most widely used by technicians to identify trends and trend reversals.

How Trendlines Are Drawn

Drawing trendlines is easy. A trendline is simply a straight line that connects a series of security prices, either tops or bottoms.

An up trendline is a straight line that connects a series of reaction lows, as illustrated in Figure 6-2. Note that the trendline appears at the bottom of the price pattern and is drawn up and to the right.

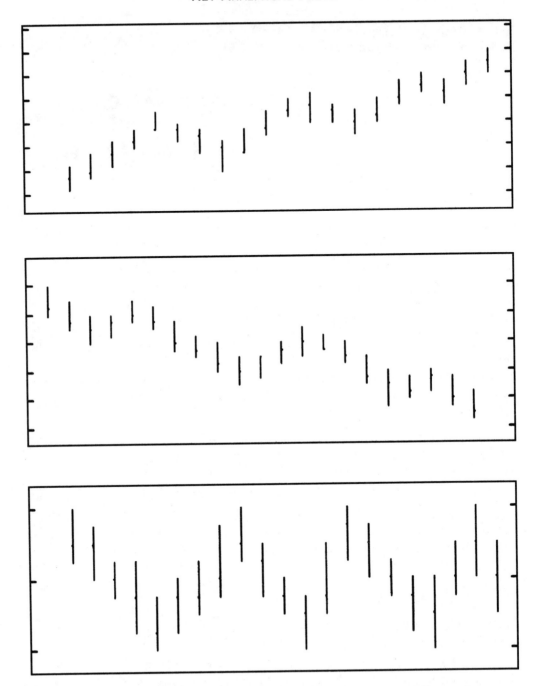

Figure 6-1   Uptrend (*top*), Downtrend (*middle*), and Sideways Trend (*bottom*)

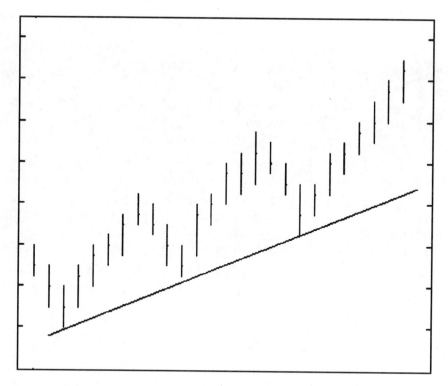

Figure 6-2   Up Trendline

A down trendline is a straight line that connects a series of rally tops, as illustrated in Figure 6-3. Note that, in this case, the trendline is at the top of the price pattern. It is drawn down and to the right.

Some guidelines to use when drawing trendlines are appropriate. First of all, there must be at least two tops or bottoms to begin a trendline. This only makes sense, because one must have two points in order to draw a straight line. Second, after drawing a trendline based on two tops or bottoms, one will frequently find that a higher top or lower bottom has been made, requiring the trendline to be redrawn.

Significance of a Trendline

The significance of a trendline is determined by two factors, namely the number of points (tops or bottoms) that the trendline goes through and the length of time the trendline has persisted without being penetrated.

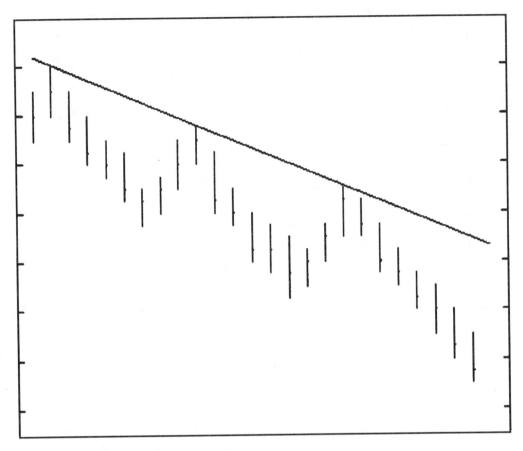

Figure 6-3   Down Trendline

Many technicians argue that although it only takes two points (tops or bottoms) to draw a trendline, connection to a third point (top or bottom) is required for the trendline to be confirmed as valid. Each time prices move back to the trendline and then renew their advance (in the case of an up trendline) or decline (in the case of a down trendline) the significance of the trendline is enhanced.

The length of the trendline indicates the period of time that prices have remained above or below the trendline. Obviously, the longer that period is, the greater the significance of the trendline. For example, a trendline that has not been penetrated for 10 months is more significant than one that has held for 10 weeks or 10 days.

In addition to the number of points that a trendline goes through and the length of time the trendline has persisted, some technicians feel the angle of the trendline adds to the significance of a trendline. In general, the closer to horizontal the trendline is, the greater the significance of any penetration through it. Very steep trendlines can easily be broken by brief sideways consolidation moves; trendlines that are less steep are not subject to many short-term price movements (that are often inconsistent with the current trend).

Validity of Trendline Penetration

Once a trendline has been established, a change in the direction of the trend is signaled by prices breaking through the trendline. In the case of an up trendline, this occurs as illustrated in Figure 6-4. Figure 6-5 shows the penetration of a down trendline.

Two criteria are used to determine the validity of a trendline penetration. The first criterion is the extent of penetration—how far prices have moved past the trendline. There is no right answer to the question: How far do prices have to move before the breaking of a trendline is considered valid? It depends to a great degree on the volatility of the security. However, some technicians use a three percent rule in regard to stocks. If the closing price for the day is three percent lower (for an up trendline) or higher (for a down trendline), then the penetration is viewed as decisive and valid. The three percent move does not have to happen in one day, although it is not unusual for prices to do so.

Some technicians also use a time filter. For example, if prices close above an up trendline or below a down trendline for two days in a row, it is viewed as a valid penetration and prices are likely to continue their reversal.

TECHNICAL ANALYSIS TIP

On occasion, prices will break through an up or down trendline on an intraday basis, but then close above (in the case of an up trendline) or below (in the case of a down trendline). Is this a trendline penetration? No, most technicians look at the closing price only for trendline penetrations. However, some would redraw the trendline so that it goes through the bottom of the intraday low (for an up trendline) or the top of the intraday high (for a down trendline).

TRENDLINE
PENETRATION

Figure 6-4   Penetration of Up Trendline

The second criterion relates to the volume. The validity of a trendline penetration is enhanced if it is accompanied by expanding volume (especially when down trendlines are broken). However, it is not essential for volume to increase for there to be a valid penetration. In other words, the extent of penetration is more important than its volume characteristics.

TECHNICAL ANALYSIS TIP

How far will prices move from a trendline once a valid penetration occurs? Typically, prices will move at least as far as the maximum distance they were on the opposite side of the trendline. For example,

TRENDLINE PENETRATION

Figure 6-5   Penetration of Down Trendline

if the price of a stock reached $100 per share before declining and breaking through an up trendline at $80 per share, you can expect prices to fall to at least $60 per share as illustrated in Figure 6-6.

Curved Trendlines

A trendline is normally thought of as a straight line connecting a series of reaction lows in an uptrend or rally highs in a downtrend. An interesting variation from the straight trendline is the curved trendline.

It is not unusual for an advance or decline in prices to rapidly pick up momentum and move away from an established trendline in a curving fashion.

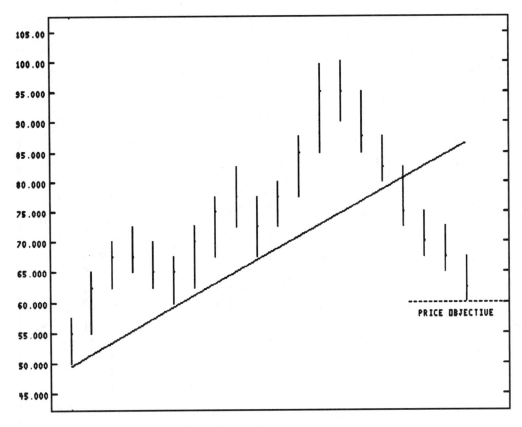

Figure 6-6   Move from Trendline after Penetration

If this curving occurs after an extended rise in prices, it signals the potential of a buying climax (blowoff). On the other hand, if the curving action happens following an extended decline in prices, it warns you of the possibility of a selling climax. In both cases, as momentum accelerates and prices move almost vertically, volume typically reaches an abnormally high level.

An upcurving trendline connects a series of reaction lows in an uptrend, while a downcurving trendline is drawn through a series of rally highs. Both can be drawn with a "French curve" (a template used to draw various curved lines).

Significant penetration of a curved trendline is as valid as that of a straight trendline. It signals a change in the direction of the trend.

Trendline Role Reversal

Once a trendline is decisively penetrated, it normally changes its role from one of support to one of resistance for an up trendline (see Figure 6-7) or resistance to support for a down trendline (see Figure 6-8). More about support and resistance is presented in Lesson 7.

Note in both Figures 6-7 and 6-8 that prices first moved away from the trendline, then back to it, then away again. This is called a *pull-back* and is not uncommon. Pull-backs offer investors great entry points for buying or selling short.

Figure 6-7   Role Reversal from Support to Resistance

Figure 6-8   Role Reversal from Resistance to Support

Trend Channels

In many instances, prices repeatedly move about the same distance away from a trendline before returning to the trendline. In these cases, a straight line can be drawn connecting the peaks of rallies in an uptrend or the bottoms of declines in a downtrend. That line is often parallel to the trendline and is called a *return* or *channel line*. Together the channel line and trendline create a trend channel, a range within which prices are moving.

Figures 6-9 and 6-10 illustrate trend channels in an uptrend and down-trend, respectively.

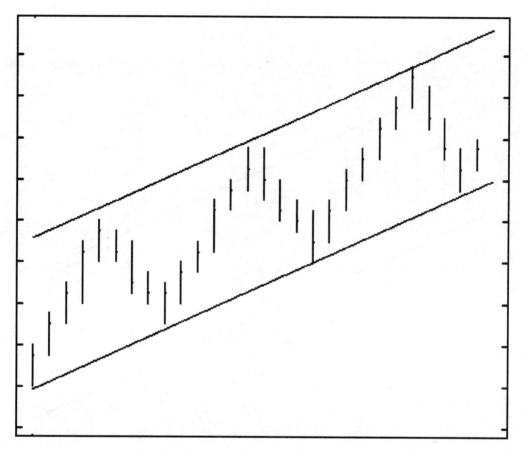

Figure 6-9 Uptrend Channel

Well-defined trend channels appear most frequently in charts of actively traded securities. Thinly traded securities offer little opportunity for trend channels to develop.

Trend channels can be used in many fashions. Novice technicians often use trend channels to determine good profit-taking levels. For example, in an uptrend, they will sell a stock when it reaches the upper level of its trend channel.

More experienced technicians watch price movements within the two boundary lines of the trend channel looking for a warning signal that the trend direction is changing. If, in an upward trend channel, prices rally up

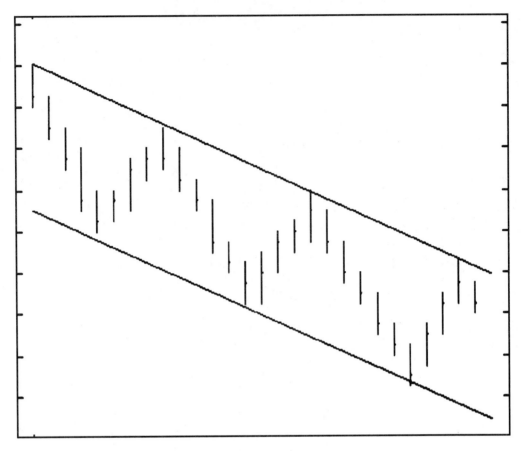

Figure 6-10   Downtrend Channel

from the trendline but fail to reach the upper channel line, it signals a deterioration of the trend and probability that the lower line will be broken.
Frequently, the distance from the top of the failed rally to the channel line
equals the distance by which the next move down penetrates the trendline.

Similarly, in a downward trend channel, if prices drop from the trendline
but fail to reach the bottom channel line, it signals a deterioration of
the trend and probability that the upper line will be broken. Likewise, the
distance from the bottom of the failed attempt to reach the channel line to the
channel line often is equal to the distance by which the next rally penetrates the trendline.

Trend channels can be used in another way. If prices break through the upper line in an upward trend channel, an acceleration of the existing uptrend is signaled. At this point, some investors will buy additional positions.

On the other hand, if prices move through the bottom line of a downward trend channel, the existing downtrend appears to be picking up pace. Short positions may be increased at this point.

The Fan Principle

One final method that uses trendlines warrants discussion. It is called the *fan principle* because it reflects the drawing of three trendlines in a fan-like appearance.

Let's examine an upward trending fan first. As illustrated in Figure 6-11, an initial trendline is drawn connecting the low prices in a normal fashion. The trendline is broken, and prices move to a lower point from which they rally back to the bottom of the trendline (which now acts as resistance instead of support). A second trendline is drawn from the low beginning of the first trendline and low of the penetration through the first trendline. Prices once again decline and break through the second trendline creating a new low. They then rally up to the bottom of the second trendline. The third and final trendline is drawn from the low beginning the first trendline and the low just created. When prices subsequently fall and break through the third trendline a reversal in prices is signaled.

A downward trending fan is illustrated in Figure 6-12. Similar to an upward trending fan, the breaking of the third trendline is what signals a reversal in prices.

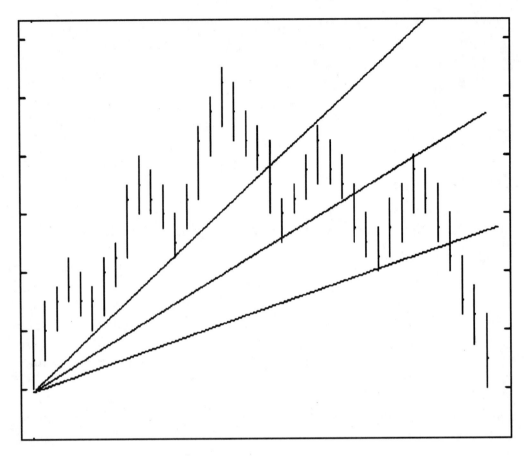

Figure 6-11   The Fan Principle—Up

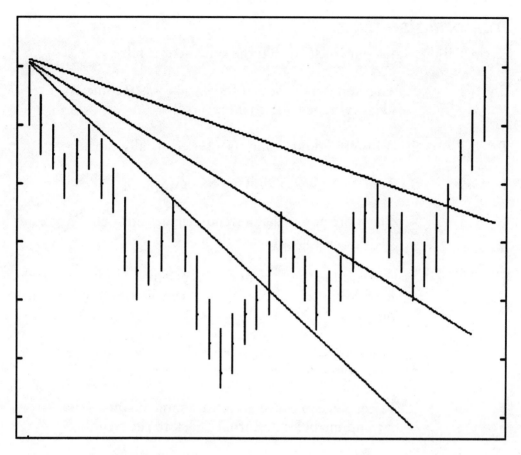

Figure 6-12   The Fan Principle—Down

True or False Quiz

Circle **T** if the statement is true or **F** if the statement is false.

T   F   1. The trendline is one of the basic tools technicians use to identify trends and trend reversals.

T   F   2. An up trendline connects a series of rally tops.

T   F   3. Trends can be up, down, or sideways.

T   F   4. The more points that a trendline goes through, the greater the significance of a trendline.

T   F   5. A trendline that has not been penetrated for 10 months is of equal technical significance to a trendline that has not been broken for 10 weeks.

T   F   6. Once an uptrend is penetrated, it normally changes its role from one of support to one of resistance.

T   F   7. Prices seldom move about the same distance away from a trendline before returning back to the trendline.

T   F   8. Trend channels appear frequently in charts of actively traded stocks.

T   F   9. Using the fan principle, a reversal in prices is signaled when prices break through the second of three trendlines.

Answers

1. *True.*
2. *False.* An up trendline connects a series of reaction lows. See Figure 6-2.
3. *True.*
4. *True.*
5. *False.* The longer the period is that prices do not penetrate a trend-line, the greater the technical significance.
6. *True.*
7. *False.* In many instances, prices repeatedly move about the same distance away from a trendline before returning back to the trendline. As a result, trend channels can be drawn as illustrated in Figure 6-9.
8. *True.*
9. *False.* Breaking of the third trendline signals a reversal in prices.

SUPPORT AND RESISTANCE

In Lesson 6, support and resistance were referred to briefly. In this lesson, the concepts of support and resistance will be more fully explained. In addition, two sophisticated applications of support and resistance, namely percentage retracements and speed resistance lines, will be examined.

Support and Resistance Defined

In the Wall Street environment, the terms *support* and *resistance* are almost synonymous with demand and supply, respectively. Support is a price level at which there is adequate demand for a security to stop its downward price movement and, normally, turn prices upward. (See Figure 7-1.) Support occurs at reaction lows.

Resistance is a price level at which there is a significant supply of a stock causing prices to halt an upward move and, typically, turn prices down. (See Figure 7-2.) Resistance occurs at reaction highs.

In an uptrend, both support and resistance levels rise as illustrated in Figure 7-3. Typically, support levels hold while resistance offers temporary halts to upward movements in prices. Resistance levels are repeatedly broken until the uptrend is reversed.

In a downtrend, both support and resistance levels move lower as illustrated in Figure 7-4. Typically, resistance levels hold while support levels temporarily stop down price movements. Support levels are repeatedly broken until the downtrend is reversed.

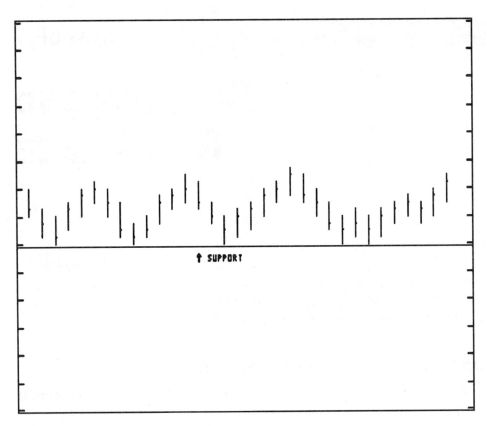

Figure 7-1   Support

TECHNICAL ANALYSIS TIP

Beware of round numbers! Technicians have discovered that prices often find support or resistance at round numbers, such as 10, 20, 25, 50, 75, 100, etc. Round numbers act as psychological levels that stop advances or declines.

As a rule, don't place trading orders or protective stop-loss orders at round numbers. In an uptrend, it is better to place buy orders just above round numbers and stop loss orders just below round numbers. On the other hand, if you want to sell short in a downtrend, place your sell order just below and your stop loss order just above the appropriate round number.

Round numbers are particularly important for short-term traders.

Role Reversal

In an uptrend, resistance levels often become support levels after they are broken significantly as illustrated in Figure 7-5. In a downtrend, the opposite occurs as support levels frequently become resistance levels. (See Figure 7-6.)

The likelihood of role reversal, from support to resistance or resistance to support, depends on three factors. First, the greater the volume that occurs at a support or resistance level, the more significant the level is and, thus, the more likely a candidate the level is for role reversal. Second, the longer that prices trade near the support or resistance level, the greater the chance of role reversal. For example, the probability of role reversal is

Figure 7-2   Resistance

Figure 7-3   Rising Support and Resistance

enhanced if consolidation occurs near a support or resistance level for a few weeks rather than a few days. Finally, the more recently that trading occurred at the level, the fresher it is in traders' minds, and the more likely it is that role reversal will occur.

Trend Reversals

In an uptrend, a trend reversal occurs when prices are held at a resistance level. A double top or some other reversal formation develops at that point and the trend changes direction as illustrated in Figure 7-7.

Figure 7-4   Declining Support and Resistance

A trend reversal occurs in a downtrend when prices are unable to penetrate a support level. In this case, a bottom reversal pattern is formed, and the trend changes direction to the upside as illustrated in Figure 7-8.

Keep in mind that a trend reversal is not signaled by the first failure to break through a resistance level (in an uptrend) or a support level (in a downtrend). A reversal pattern must fully develop before one gets the signal that the trend has changed. In other words, a trader should not rush to sell all of his or her securities or sell short just because prices have held at a resistance level. Likewise, one should not load up on securities or cover short positions just because prices initially fail to penetrate a support level. Wait for more evidence that a trend reversal is occurring.

Percentage Retracements

After prices move either up or down for a period of time, they usually move in the opposite direction, retracing a portion of the previous move. Subsequently, prices continue in the original trend direction.

Countertrend price moves frequently move by a percentage range amount. Often prices will retrace from a minimum of one-third (or 33 percent) to a maximum of two-thirds (67 percent) of its previous move before continuing in its original trend direction. Figure 7-9 illustrates a 50 percent retracement which is very common.

Some traders view a retracement of 33 percent to 50 percent as a buying opportunity in an uptrend or a selling opportunity in a downtrend. The

Figure 7-5   Uptrend Role Reversal from Resistance to Support

two-thirds level is a critical area. If prices move past the two-thirds retracement level, a trend reversal is likely.

Speed Resistance Lines

Speed resistance lines (also known as speed lines) are based on a theory that trends are divided into thirds. Unlike percentage retracements that look at just price movements in terms of thirds, speed resistance lines look at both price and time. Speed resistance lines measure the rate at which a trend moves up or down.

In an uptrend, speed resistance lines are constructed by dividing the vertical distance from the beginning of the trend to the highest point on the

Figure 7-6 Downtrend Role Reversal from Support to Resistance

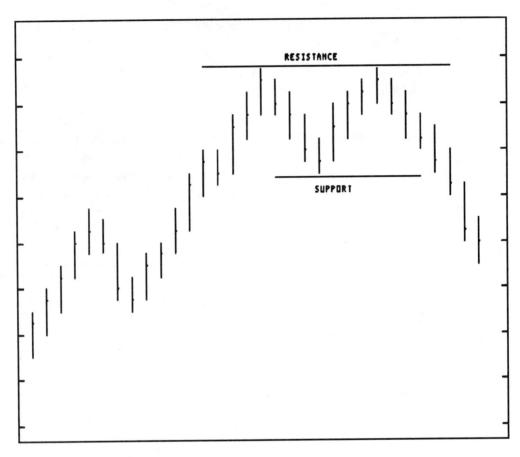

Figure 7-7   Trend Reversal at Top

chart. That distance is then divided into thirds. Two trendlines are drawn as illustrated in Figure 7-10. The first trendline is drawn from the beginning of the trend to one-third of the way up the vertical distance. The second trendline is drawn from the beginning of the trend to two-thirds of the way up the vertical distance.

Figure 7-11 illustrates the construction of speed resistance lines in a downtrend. The principles are similar to those used in construction of speed resistance lines in an uptrend.

How do you use speed resistance lines? It is simple.

If, in an uptrend, prices have made a new peak and are retracing (or correcting) some of the upward movement, they will frequently stop at the

RESISTANCE

SUPPORT

Figure 7-8   Trend Reversal at Bottom

two-thirds speed resistance line. If prices do not stop at the two-thirds line, they will probably move to the one-third speed resistance line. If they are not held at the one-third line, a trend reversal is signaled.

In a downtrend, breaking the two-thirds speed resistance line suggests the likelihood of a rally to the one-third line. If that is penetrated, a trend reversal is probable.

Figure 7-9   Example of Percentage Retracement

Figure 7-10   Speed Resistance Lines in an Uptrend

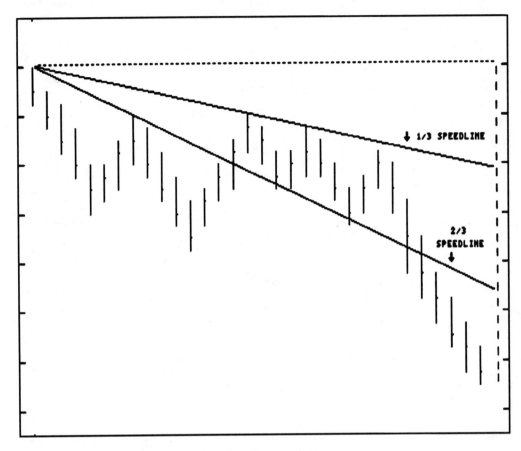

Figure 7-11   Speed Resistance Lines in a Downtrend

True or False Quiz

Circle T if the statement is true or F if the statement is false.

T   F   1. Support occurs at reaction lows, while resistance occurs at reaction highs.

T   F   2. In a downtrend, support levels are repeatedly broken until a reversal in prices occurs.

T   F   3. Prices seldom find support or resistance at round numbers.

T   F   4. Support levels never become resistance levels.

T   F   5. In an uptrend, a trend reversal occurs when prices are held at a resistance level.

T   F   6. Percentage retracements examine countertrend price moves in terms of thirds.

T   F   7. If prices break the two-thirds speed resistance line, the probability is that they will continue to the one-third speed resistance line.

Answers

1. *True.*
2. *True.*
3. *False.* Prices often find support or resistance at round numbers.
4. *False.* In a downtrend support levels frequently become resistance levels. See Figure 7-6.
5. *True.* See Figure 7-7.
6. *True.*
7. *True.*

THE TRUE VALUE OF FAILED SIGNALS

In Lessons 3 through 7, you learned about a wide variety of chart patterns, as well as trendlines, and support and resistance. Typically, prices will follow through in the direction that they break through a boundary line of a given chart pattern, cross over a trendline, move above a resistance level, or decline below a support level. However, that does not always happen.

What should you do when prices fail to follow through in the direction indicated by a price breakout? Experienced technicians know that a failed signal is one of the most reliable of all chart signals. When prices fail to follow through in the direction of a price breakout, there is a high probability of a significant move in the opposite direction.

Skilled technicians recognize the true value of failed signals and are not only able to exit a losing trade, but to do a 180-degree turn and enter a trade in the opposite direction. Discipline is required to take advantage of failed signals, but taking quick action can prove to be very profitable. Let's look at three examples.

Bull Trap

Figure 8-1 presents an example of a *bull trap* in the trading of Scientific Atlanta. Prices broke out of a symmetrical triangle chart pattern to the upside signaling higher prices. However, after a brief move to the upside, prices reentered the symmetrical triangle and moved quickly through it and sharply lower.

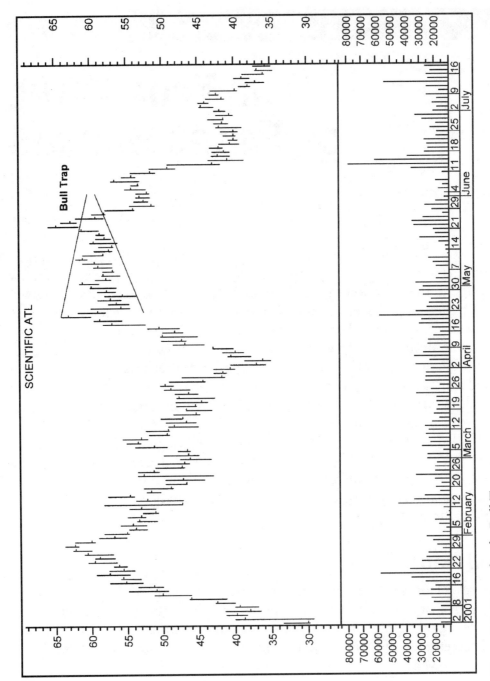

Figure 8-1 Example of a Bull Trap

This type of failed signal is known as a bull trap since it leaves those who were bullish, having bought on the upside breakout, with losses. The higher the volume in the trap, the more bulls were caught.

Bear Trap

The *bear trap* is less common than the bull trap. It occurs when prices break out on the downside from a trading range or other chart pattern and then rally back up through the top of the trading range or upper boundary line of a chart pattern. Similar to the bull trap, the higher the volume in the trap, the more bears are caught.

Figure 8-2 provides an example of a bear trap in the trading of General Dynamics. After prices established a trading range, prices penetrated the lower boundary line. However, they were unable to follow through to the downside. Subsequently, a reversal occurred and prices moved significantly higher up through the top of the trading range.

Failed Trendline Signals

Trendlines are one of the most often used tools in the technician's toolbox. They are also particularly prone to false breakouts. It is not unusual for slight penetrations of trendlines to occur with no follow through. For that reason, many technicians use time and price filters before recognizing trendline breakouts as legitimate. A time filter means that prices must remain above or below the trendline for a certain number of periods, while a price filter requires that prices move a minimum of a certain amount or percentage away from the trendline before accepting the signal.

Even if you use time or price filters, there will still be failed trendline signals that offer profit-making opportunities, since prices tend to move dramatically in the opposite direction of the signal shortly thereafter. Figure 8-3 illustrates a failed trendline signal that occurred in the Standard & Poor's 500 Index. A downside breakout of an up trendline defined by three prior relative lows was soon followed by prices rising back through the trendline. Subsequently, prices climbed sharply higher.

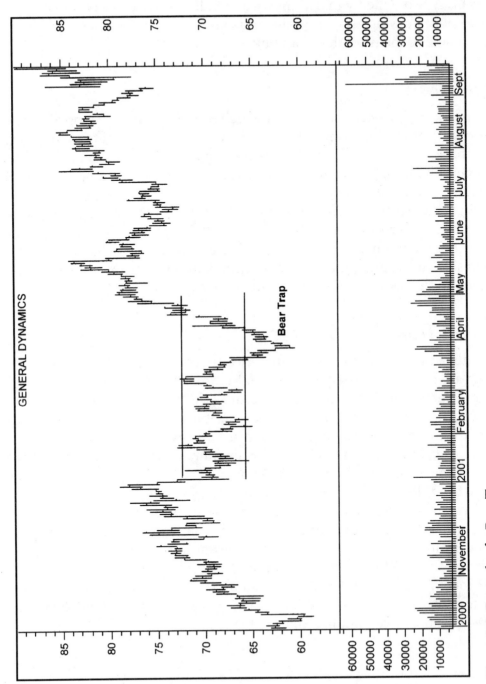

Figure 8-2 Example of a Bear Trap

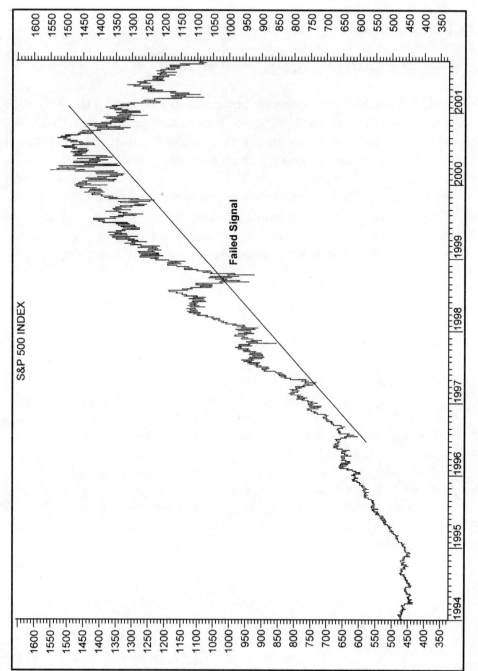

Figure 8-3 Example of a Failed Trendline Signal

True or False Quiz

Circle **T** if the statement is true or **F** if the statement is false.

T   F   1. Chart pattern signals are always right.

T   F   2. A bull trap occurs when prices break out on the downside from a trading range or other chart pattern and then rally back up through the top of the trading range or upper boundary line of a chart pattern.

T   F   3. Typically, the higher the volume associated with a bear trap, the more bears are caught.

T   F   4. Trendlines are particularly prone to false breakouts.

Answers

1. *False.* While chart pattern signals are typically right, they are not always right.
2. *False.* A bear trap occurs when prices break out on the downside from a trading range or other chart pattern and then rally back up through the top of the trading range or upper boundary line of a chart pattern.
3. *True.*
4. *True.*

USING MOVING AVERAGES

One of the most widely used tools in the technician's toolbox is the *moving average*. Various types of moving averages are used to smooth price fluctuations and get a clearer picture of a security's price trend.

This lesson will show the advantages and disadvantages of simple, weighted, and exponential moving averages. It will teach how to use one moving average or two or more in combination to signal the trend of prices. In addition, the envelope (also known as a *trading band*), a moving average filter, will be discussed.

Before discussing the types of moving averages, it is important to understand exactly what a moving average is. An average is the sum of whatever you are examining (for example, the closing prices of a stock) for a number of instances (for example, 10 days) divided by the number of instances (10 days). The moving part of moving average means that one recalculates the average for each additional instance (day).

Simple Moving Average

The simple moving average is used by many technicians because it is the easiest type of moving average to calculate, and it is fairly effective. It is equivalent to the moving arithmetic mean.

The simple moving average is calculated by adding the prices (typically closing prices) for a number of periods (hours, days, weeks, etc.) and dividing by the number of periods. Let's look at an example. Table 9-1 shows sample closing price data for 20 days, as well as how to calculate a five-day simple moving average. You simply add up the last five days' closing prices and divide by five.

Figure 9-1 shows the five-day simple moving average plotted on a bar chart. Note that there is no simple moving average charted for the first four days, since there are not enough data to make the calculation until the fifth day.

Longer time periods are typically used for simple moving averages. For example, the commonly used 200-day simple moving average of the Standard & Poor's 500 Index closing prices is plotted in Figure 9-2. As a rule of thumb, as long as the Index is above its 200-day simple moving average, the outlook is bullish. On the other hand, when it falls below its 200-day simple moving average, it is a bearish sign.

Table 9-1 Calculating a Five-Day Simple Moving Average

Date	Closing Price	Five-Day Total (A)	Five-Day Simple Moving Average (A)/5
March 22	45.375		
March 23	45.500		
March 24	45.000		
March 25	43.625		
March 28	43.375 222.875	44.575	
March 29	43.125	220.625	44.125
March 30	43.125	218.250	43.650
March 31	44.250	217.500	43.500
April 4	43.500	217.375	43.475
April 5	44.375	218.375	43.675
April 6	45.875	221.125	44.225
April 7	46.750	224.750	44.950
April 8	47.625	228.125	45.625
April 11	48.000	232.625	46.525
April 12	49.125	237.375	47.475
April 13	48.750	240.250	48.050
April 14	46.125	239.625	47.925
April 15	46.750	238.750	47.750
April 18	46.625	237.375	47.475
April 19	46.000	234.250	46.850

A major criticism of the simple moving average is that it gives equal weight to each period's price rather than weighting recent periods' action heavier than older periods' price action. Both weighted and exponential moving averages answer that criticism.

TECHNICAL ANALYSIS TIP

Recalculating simple moving averages on a daily (or other period) basis is easy. Suppose you are calculating a 50-day simple moving average. You don't have to add up the prices for 50 days every day. Here's how you do it and save a lot of time.

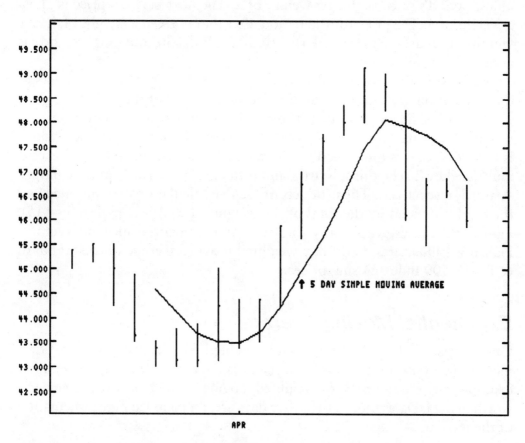

Figure 9-1 Five-Day Simple Moving Average of Example Data

> *The first day you add up the 50 prices. Write down your total before you divide by 50 to calculate the average. The second day take that total, add the new day's price, and subtract the oldest day's price (50 days ago). Then divide by 50.*
>
> *Repeat the process on a daily basis.*

Weighted Moving Average

The weighted moving average gives each period's price a "weight" based on its age. The oldest period's price is given a weight of 1. The next to the oldest period's price is given a weight of 2. The next period's price is given a weight of 3. The price for the period after that is given a weight of 4. The weight increases by 1 until the final period (the current period) is assigned a weight.

Each period's price is multiplied by the given weight. The products of the calculation are summed and divided by the total of the weights.

Let's look at an example. Table 9-2 illustrates the calculation of a weighted moving average for a five-day period. The first day's price, which is the oldest day, is multiplied by the weight of 1. The second day's price is multiplied by 2. The third, fourth, and fifth days' prices are multiplied by 3, 4, and 5, respectively. The products of the five calculations are summed and the total is divided by the total of the weights $(1 + 2 + 3 + 4 + 5 = 15)$. Figure 9-3 shows graphically the five-day exponential moving average. Figure 9-4 illustrates a 200-day weighted moving average of the Standard & Poor's 500 Index closing prices.

Exponential Moving Average

One criticism of both the simple and weighted moving average is that they include data for only the number of periods the moving average covers. For example, a five-day simple or weighted moving average only uses five days' worth of data. Data prior to those five days are not included in the calculation of the moving average.

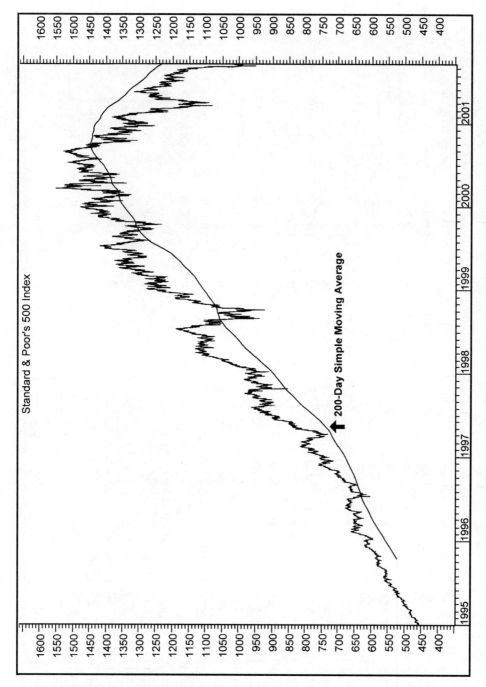

Figure 9-2   200-Day Simple Moving Average of the Standard & Poor's 500 Index Closing Prices

Table 9-2   Calculating a Five-Day Weighted Moving Average

Date	Closing Price	Closing Price Four Days Ago Times 1 (A)	Closing Price Three Days Ago Times 2 (B)	Closing Price Two Days Ago Times 3 (C)	Closing Price One Day Ago Times 4 (D)	Today's Closing Price Times 5 (E)	Five-day Total of Closing Prices Times Weightings (A + B + C + D + E) = (F)	Five-day Weighted Moving Average (F)/15
03/22	45.375							
03/23	45.500							
03/24	45.000							
03/25	43.625							
03/28	43.375	45.375	91.000	135.000	174.500	216.875	662.750	44.183
03/29	43.125	45.500	90.000	130.875	173.500	215.625	655.500	43.700
03/30	43.125	45.000	87.250	130.125	172.500	215.625	650.500	43.367
03/31	44.250	43.625	86.750	129.375	172.500	221.250	653.500	43.567
04/04	43.500	43.375	86.250	129.375	177.000	217.500	653.500	43.567
04/05	44.375	43.125	86.250	132.750	174.000	221.875	658.000	43.867
04/06	45.875	43.125	88.500	130.500	177.500	229.375	669.000	44.600
04/07	46.750	44.250	87.000	133.125	183.500	233.750	681.625	45.442
04/08	47.625	43.500	88.750	137.625	187.000	238.125	695.000	46.333
04/11	48.000	44.375	91.750	140.250	190.500	240.000	706.875	47.125
04/12	49.125	45.875	93.500	142.875	192.000	245.625	719.875	47.992
04/13	48.750	46.750	95.250	144.000	196.500	243.750	726.250	48.417
04/14	46.125	47.625	96.000	147.375	195.000	230.625	716.625	47.775
04/15	46.750	48.000	98.250	146.250	184.500	233.750	710.750	47.383
04/18	46.625	49.125	97.500	138.375	187.000	233.125	705.125	47.008
04/19	46.000	48.750	92.250	140.250	186.500	230.000	697.750	46.517

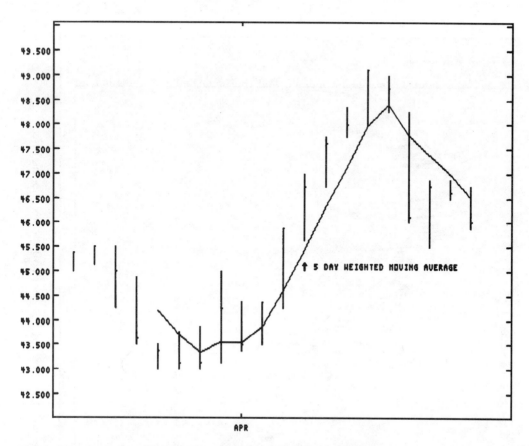

Figure 9-3   Five-Day Weighted Moving Average of Example Data

TECHNICAL ANALYSIS TIP

How many periods should you use when calculating a moving average? There is no magic answer. The "best" number of periods to use varies significantly from security to security and depends on your investment time horizon (short-, intermediate-, or long-term). You will have to test a number of different periods for each security you are examining to determine an optimal number of periods to use in calculating a moving average.

As a rule of thumb, the shorter the average, the greater the number of trend signals (including false ones).

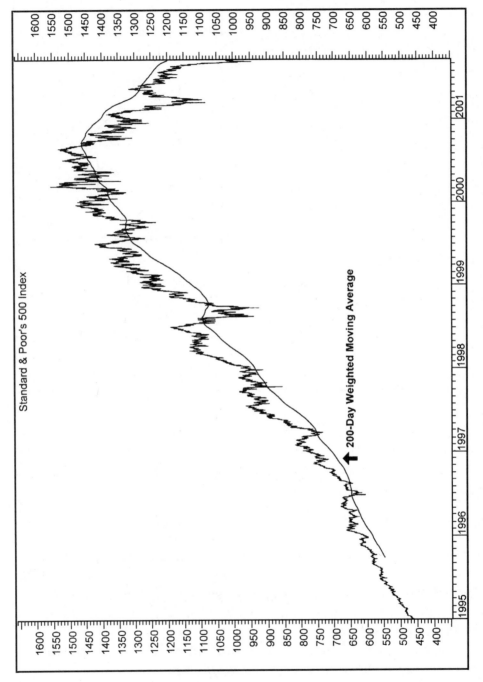

Figure 9-4 200-Day Weighted Moving Average of the Standard & Poor's 500 Index Closing Prices

130

Many technicians believe that the prior data is an important reflection of prices and should be included (on a weighted basis with older data given less weight) in a moving average calculation. These technicians frequently use an exponential moving average to accomplish that task.

An exponential moving average gives more weight to recent prices and ever-decreasing weight to older data. Unlike simple and weighted moving averages, the older data never goes away in the calculation of exponential moving averages.

The formula for calculating exponential moving averages is somewhat complex and is best done with the aid of a computer. However, let's look at a basic example in order to show, in principle, how it is calculated.

Table 9-3 illustrates the calculation of a five-day exponential moving average of closing prices. Before calculating the exponential moving average on a daily basis, you must have a beginning moving average number (previous day's exponential moving average). To start, use a five-day simple moving average for the previous day's exponential moving average. Each day you make the following calculation: The previous day's exponential moving average is subtracted from the current day's closing price. That difference is multiplied by the exponential moving average exponent (in this case, 0.4) to arrive at a number that is added (or subtracted, if negative) to the previous day's exponential moving average resulting in the current day's exponential moving average.

The exponent for a given time period is calculated by dividing 2 by the number of time periods in the exponential moving average. Thus, for five periods, the exponential equals 2 divided by 5 or 0.4. Some other examples of exponents follow:

Number of Periods	Exponent
10	0.2
20	0.1
50	0.04
200	0.01

Figure 9-5 shows graphically a five-day exponential moving average of the data presented in Table 9-3.

Figure 9-6 illustrates a 200-day exponential moving average of the Standard & Poor's 500 Index closing prices.

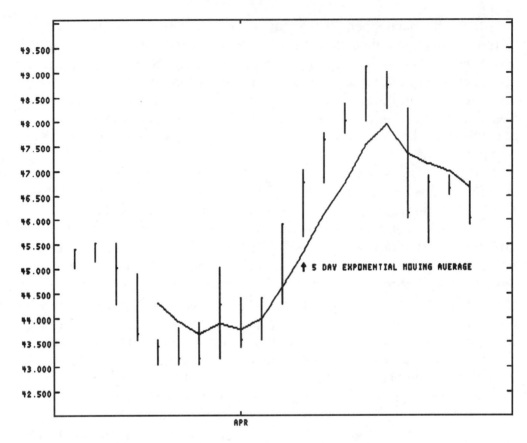

Figure 9-5   Five-Day Exponential Moving Average of Example Data

---

TECHNICAL ANALYSIS TIP

Which type of moving average—simple, weighted, or exponential—is best? There is no correct answer. In many cases, a simple moving average will work just as well as the much more difficult to calculate exponential moving average. However, as a rule, the exponential moving average is more sensitive to changes in price than the simple moving average, but less than the weighted moving average. Once again, you must experiment to see which type of moving average (as well as which number of periods of time) will work best with the investment opportunity you are analyzing.

Table 9-3 Calculating a Five-Day Exponential Moving Average

Date	Closing Price (A)	Previous Day's EMA (B)	Closing Price Minus Previous Day's EMA (A) − (B) = (C)	Difference Times Smoothing Constant (C) × 0.4 = (D)	Five-Day EMA Previous Day's EMA + (D)
March 22	45.375				
March 23	45.500				
March 24	45.000				
March 25	43.625				
March 28	43.375	44.575*	−1.200	−0.480	44.095
March 29	43.125	44.095	−0.970	−0.388	43.707
March 30	43.125	43.707	−0.582	−0.233	43.474
March 31	44.250	43.474	0.776	0.310	43.785
April 4	43.500	43.785	−0.285	−0.114	43.671
April 5	44.375	43.671	0.704	0.282	43.952
April 6	45.875	43.952	1.923	0.769	44.721
April 7	46.750	44.721	2.029	0.811	45.533
April 8	47.625	45.533	2.092	0.837	46.370
April 11	48.000	46.370	1.630	0.652	47.022
April 12	49.125	47.022	2.103	0.841	47.863
April 13	48.750	47.863	0.887	0.355	48.218
April 14	46.125	48.218	−2.093	−0.837	47.381
Apri l15	46.750	47.381	−0.631	−0.252	47.128
April 18	46.625	47.128	−0.503	−0.201	46.927
April 19	46.000	46.927	−0.927	−0.371	46.556

*Five-day simple moving average.

Multiple Moving Averages

Moving averages of differing lengths are often used together in trend determination. The objective of using more than one moving average is to reduce whipsaw trades.

When two moving averages are used, a buy signal is given when the shorter-term moving average crosses above the longer-term moving average. A sell signal occurs when the opposite happens: the longer-term moving

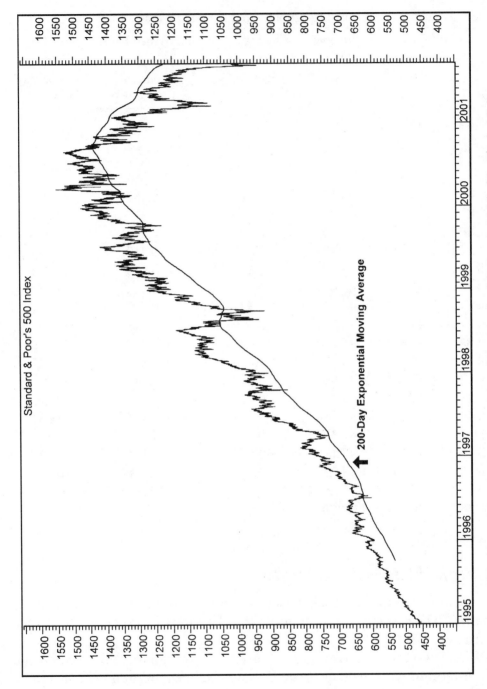

Figure 9-6   200-Day Exponential Moving Average of the Standard & Poor's 500 Index Closing Prices average crosses above the shorter-term moving average. Figure 9-7 shows 5- and 20-day simple moving averages for PepsiCo and the signals they generate in combination. Note that the shorter 5-day simple moving average is much more sensitive to trend changes than the longer 20-day simple moving average. Three moving averages can also be used in a triple crossover method. A popular combination employs 4-, 9-, and 18-day moving averages. It is principally used with commodities. A buy signal is generated when both the 4-(acts as a warning) and 9-(acts as a confirmation) day moving averages cross above the 18-day moving average. Sell signals are produced by the crossing of the 4- and 9-day moving averages below the 18-day moving average.

Envelopes (Trading Bands)

Envelopes (also known as trading bands) create a filter around a moving average line. Two lines, one above and one below, are drawn parallel to the moving average. The distance between the moving average and the upper and lower envelope lines is a certain percentage. That percentage amount depends on the particular trading technique one is employing.

One common use of envelopes is to signal when prices are particularly strong or weak. For example, Figure 9-8 shows Standard & Poor's 500 Index daily data with a 21-day simple moving average line and envelope lines at 5 percent above and below the moving average line. The vast majority of the time, prices trade within plus or minus 5 percent of the moving average line. When prices break above the upper envelope line, prices are accelerating faster than normal, implying great market strength and a continued move upward in prices. When, on the other hand, prices fall below the lower envelope line, great market weakness is suggested, as well as a further decline in prices.

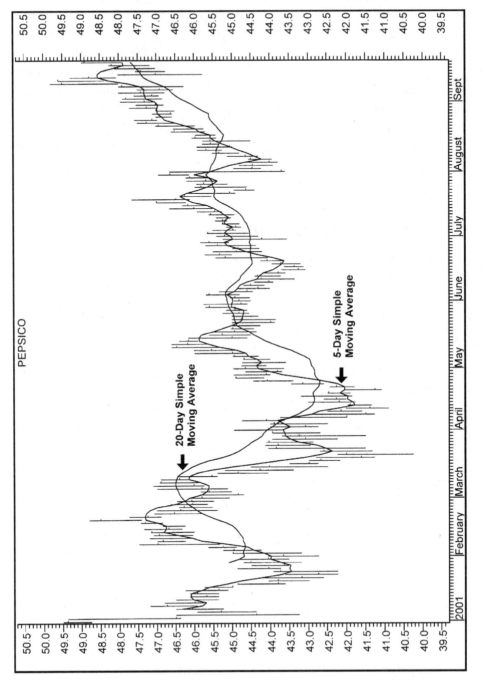

Figure 9-7   Comparison of 5- and 20-Day Simple Moving Averages for PepsiCo

136

Figure 9-8   Five Percent Envelope Around a 21-Day Simple Moving Average of the Standard & Poor's 500 Index

True or False Quiz

Circle **T** if the statement is true or **F** if the statement is false.

T   F   1. The weighted moving average is the easiest type of moving average to calculate.

T   F   2. The simple moving average gives equal weight to each period's price.

T   F   3. When prices are above a moving average line, it is generally viewed as bullish.

T   F   4. When calculating a weighted moving average, older periods' prices are given more weight than more current periods' prices.

T   F   5. A five-day weighted moving average will normally generate more signals than a 50-day weighted moving average.

T   F   6. Unlike simple and weighted moving averages, older data never go away in the calculation of exponential moving averages.

T   F   7. Normally, the simple moving average is more sensitive to price changes than the exponential moving average.

T   F   8. When two moving averages are used, a buy signal is given when the shorter-term moving average crosses above the longer-term moving average.

T   F   9. When using a combination of 4-, 9-, and 18-day moving averages, a buy signal is produced by a crossing of both the 4- and the 9-day moving averages below the 18-day moving average.

T   F   10. Envelopes are two lines, one above and one below, drawn parallel to the moving average.

Answers

1. *False.* The simple moving average is the easiest type of moving average to calculate.
2. *True.*
3. *True.*
4. *False.* Older periods' prices are given less weight than more current periods' prices in the calculation of a weighted moving average.
5. *True.*
6. *True.*
7. *False.* Since it gives more weight to the latest prices, the exponential moving average is normally more sensitive to price changes than the simple moving average.
8. *True.*
9. *False.* A buy signal is generated when both the 4- and 9-day moving averages cross above the 18-day moving average. A sell signal is produced by a crossing of both the 4- and 9-day moving averages below the 18-day moving average.
10. *True.*

RELATIVE STRENGTH ANALYSIS

Relative strength analysis is an easy concept to understand. It simply compares the performance of one item (such as a stock) with another item (such as an industry group). The objective is to determine if the first item's price is advancing or declining faster than the second item's price. In other words, is the first item outperforming or underperforming the second item on a relative basis? Relative strength analysis is normally used to compare an industry group's performance to the overall market or a particular stock's performance to its industry group. However, it can also be used to compare virtually any two items as long as they have prices (such as two stocks, two commodities, two industry groups, etc.).

Industry Group versus a Market Index

Technicians compare industry groups to the market as a whole using relative strength analysis to determine which industry groups are outperforming or underperforming the overall market. A ranking of the various industry groups can be made according to their relative strength. Those industry groups with the highest rankings are candidates for buying; whereas those with low rankings represent potential selling or short sales.

Figure 10-1 compares the savings and loan companies industry group to the Standard & Poor's 500 Index. Note that the industry's relative strength rose throughout most of the time period shown. Therefore, it was outperforming the market.

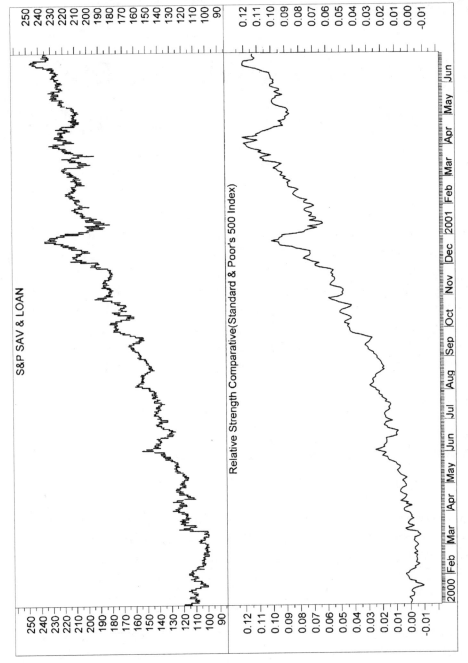

Figure 10-1 Savings and Loan Companies Industry Group (*top*) and Relative Strength of the Savings and Loan Companies Industry Group versus the Standard & Poor's 500 Index (*bottom*)

Figure 10-2 demonstrates an industry group (communications equipment) with declining relative strength when compared to the Standard & Poor's 500 Index. Thus, it was underperforming the market as a whole for the time period shown.

TECHNICAL ANALYSIS TIP

Use a top down approach when performing relative strength analysis. First, determine which industry groups are outperforming the overall market. Then, determine which stocks in the highest ranking industry group are outperforming the industry group. Finally, use the various entry technical analysis tools (such as chart patterns, moving averages, etc.) to find a good time to buy one or more of the stocks that have demonstrated strength by outperforming others.

Individual Stock versus an Industry Group

In a fashion similar to comparing an industry group to the overall market, a technician can use relative strength analysis to compare an individual stock's price performance to that of the industry to which it belongs.

Let's look at an example. Figure 10-3 compares the performance of Washington Mutual to the savings and loan companies industry group. The rising relative strength of the stock when compared to the industry as a whole throughout much of the time period shown suggests the stock's performance had been relatively strong. It could have been considered for purchase in an uptrend.

On the other hand, stocks with low relative strengths when compared to industry groups or the overall stock market may represent good short selling opportunities.

Keep in mind the old Wall Street saying "the trend is your friend." Don't buy stocks just because their relative strength is high or sell stocks solely on the basis of low relative strengths. Look at the overall trend of the market. In an uptrend, buy high relative strength stocks. In a downtrend, sell or sell short low relative strength stocks.

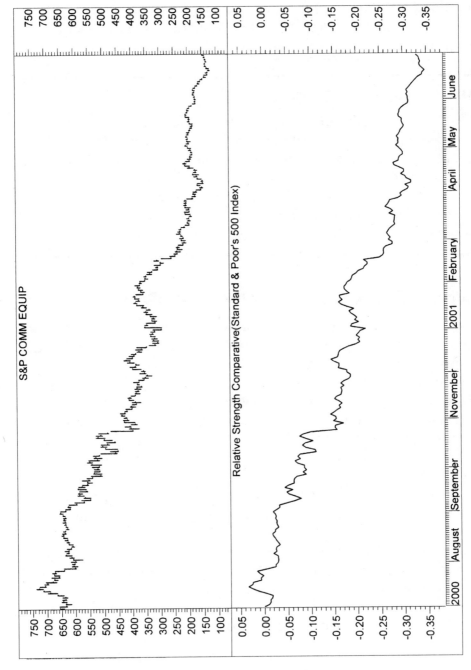

Figure 10-2 Communications Equipment Industry Group (*top*) and Relative Strength of the Communications Equipment Industry Group versus the Standard & Poor's 500 Index (*bottom*)

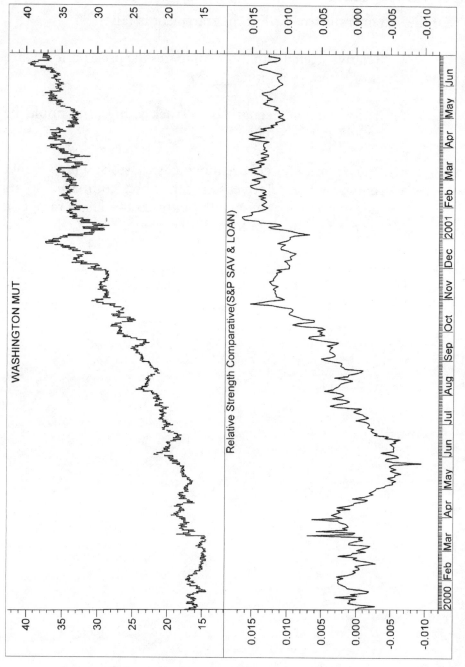

Figure 10-3 Washington Mutual (*top*) and Relative Strength of Washington Mutual versus the Savings and Loan Companies Industry Group (*bottom*)

True or False Quiz

Circle **T** if the statement is true or **F** if the statement is false.

T   F   1. Relative strength analysis compares the price performance of one item to another.

T   F   2. If the relative strength of a stock is high, it should be bought immediately.

T   F   3. When market prices are moving up, a stock with a higher than average relative strength when compared to its industry group is moving up in price at a faster rate than the average stock in its industry group.

Answers

1. *True.*
2. *False.* Even if the relative strength of a stock is high, one should perform further analysis to determine if the market is in an uptrend and use the various technical analysis tools to find a good entry time to buy the stock. Don't forget, if the overall market is going down, the probability is very high that the stock being examined is going down too (regardless of how high its relative strength is).
3. *True.*

VOLUME AND OPEN INTEREST

The majority of what was presented in the lessons thus far has related to two dimensions of market analysis, namely time and price. Most technicians examine a third dimension, which is *volume*. In addition, commodity traders analyze open interest numbers for supply and demand considerations.

Basic Rules of Volume

Historically, volume has related to market prices as follows:

Price	Volume	Implication
Rising	Up	Bullish
Rising	Down	Bearish
Declining	Up	Bearish
Declining	Down	Bullish

Volume is viewed as a measure of market strength or weakness. If volume is increasing while prices are moving either up or down, it is likely that prices will continue their current price trend. On the other hand, a decline in volume is considered to signal that steam is running out in the direction of the current trend and consolidation or a reversal could be forthcoming.

TECHNICAL ANALYSIS TIP

The widespread use of derivative market instruments has, at least temporarily, diminished the value of volume indicators. That doesn't mean you shouldn't examine them. Just view them with a grain of salt—they are not as reliable as they once were.

Blowoffs and Selling Climaxes

Dramatic market action that is common at market tops and bottoms is known as *blowoffs* and *selling climaxes*.

Blowoffs occur at market tops. They usually occur after prices have moved higher over an extended period of time. At the end of the up move, prices rally sharply accompanied by a large increase in volume. Typically, all of those that were going to buy at this level have done so. Profit taking occurs and prices reverse, often suddenly, to the downside.

Selling climaxes are simply the opposite of blowoffs. They occur at market bottoms after prices have been declining for an extended period of time. One final wave of selling drives prices sharply lower on significantly increased volume. Bargain hunters then jump in buying, reversing the trend, and sending prices higher.

On-Balance Volume

On-Balance Volume is a technique of volume analysis that has been popularized by Joseph E. Granville, author of *A New Strategy of Daily Stock Market Timing for Maximum Profit* (Prentice-Hall, Englewood Cliffs, NJ, 1976).

On-Balance Volume is calculated in two steps. First, each day's total volume is deemed as being positive or negative depending on whether prices closed higher or lower for the day. If prices close higher, the total volume is positive; if prices close lower, the total volume is negative. Second, each day's positive or negative value is summed in a running cumulative total.

The actual value of On-Balance Volume is not important. Its direction relative to market price provides clues to buying and selling pressure. (See Figure 11-1 for an example.)

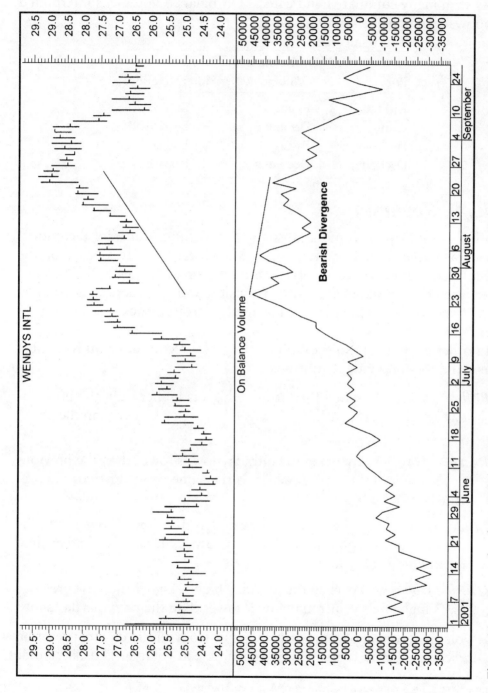

Figure 11-1   Example of On-Balance Volume: Wendy's International Price Chart (*top*) versus On-Balance Volume Chart for Wendy's International (*bottom*)

As with many cumulative indicators, On-Balance Volume is interpreted as follows using divergence analysis:

Price	On-Balance Volume	Interpretation
Rising	Rising	Bullish
Rising	Declining	Bearish
Declining	Rising	Bullish
Declining	Declining	Bearish

Volume Reversal

Another method of volume analysis is the *Volume Reversal* technique, which was implemented and refined by Mark Leibovit.* It is based on the concept that volume precedes price and, therefore, changes in the trend of prices often can be signaled by the expansion and contraction of volume. The Volume Reversal technique can be used to project stock, commodity, or index futures prices.

In order to understand the Volume Reversal technique, you first must understand the following definitions:

Rally Day—A day when the intraday high is higher than the previous day's high and the intraday low is the same or higher than the previous day's low.

Reaction Day—A day when the intraday low is lower than the previous day's low and the intraday high is the same or lower than the previous day's high.

Inside Day—A day when the intraday high is the same or lower than the previous day's high and the intraday low is the same or higher than the previous day's low.

Outside Day—A day when the intraday high is higher than the previous day's high and the intraday low is lower than the previous day's low.

A Volume Reversal occurs when a change from a rally day to a reaction day, or vice versa, is accompanied by an increase in volume. Thus, if volume

*Volume Reversal is a registered trademark of Almarco Trading Corporation.

increases and the criteria for a reaction day are met, it is considered a negative Volume Reversal and time to sell. If, on the other hand, volume increases and the criteria for a rally day are met, it is considered a positive Volume Reversal and time to buy. Inside and outside days are ignored in the Volume Reversal technique.

Let's look at two examples, one illustrating a negative Volume Reversal and one showing a positive Volume Reversal.

Example 1
Negative Volume Reversal

Day	High	Low	Close	Volume
1	$29.36	$27.18	$28.68	154,000
2	29.53	27.59	28.62	151,000
3	29.54	27.40	27.85	125,000
4	28.41	26.76	27.73	173,000

In Example 1, note that Day 2 was a rally day (higher high and higher low) followed by an outside day (higher high and lower low) on Day 3. On Day 4, a reaction day (lower high and lower low) occurred accompanied by an increase in volume signaling a negative Volume Reversal and time to sell.

Example 2
Positive Volume Reversal

Day	High	Low	Close	Volume
1	$14.58	$12.87	$13.42	89,000
2	14.23	11.50	13.46	90,000
3	16.71	13.70	16.51	100,000

In Example 2, a positive Volume Reversal signaled that it was time to buy. Day 2 was a reaction day (lower high and lower low) immediately followed on Day 3 by a rally day (higher high and higher low) accompanied by greater volume.

One final point: The closing price is not used in the Volume Reversal technique. The technique assumes that the range between the low and the high of a day gives a better indication of what actually is happening than the price at the end of the day.

Open Interest

Open interest is the number of contracts that are trading for a particular commodity. The basic rules for open interest are similar to those for volume. They are as follows:

Price	Open Interest	Interpretation
Rising	Up	Bullish
Rising	Down	Bearish
Declining	Up	Bearish
Declining	Down	Bullish

Expanding open interest in an uptrend represents aggressive new buying and is bullish. On the other hand, expanding open interest in a downtrend represents aggressive new short selling and is bearish.

Declining open interest in an uptrend represents short covering, not new buying, and is bearish. However, declining open interest in a downtrend suggests the liquidation of losing long positions and is bullish.

TECHNICAL ANALYSIS TIP

At the end of an up move in prices, a leveling off or decline in open interest should serve as a warning that a reversal in the trend of prices is forthcoming.

True or False Quiz

Circle **T** if the statement is true or **F** if the statement is false.

T   F   1. If a stock's price is rising accompanied by increasing volume, it is viewed as bullish.

T   F   2. If a stock's price is declining accompanied by increasing volume, it is viewed as bullish.

T   F   3. Blowoffs occur at market bottoms when a final wave of selling drives prices sharply lower on significantly increased volume.

T   F   4. Divergence analysis is used to interpret On-Balance Volume as bullish or bearish for prices.

T   F   5. A positive Volume Reversal occurs when volume increases and the criteria for a rally day are met.

T   F   6. Expanding open interest in a downtrend represents aggressive new buying and is bullish.

Answers

1. *True.*
2. *False.* If a stock's price is declining on increasing volume, it is considered bearish.
3. *False.* Selling climaxes occur at market bottoms; blowoffs occur at market tops.
4. *True.*
5. *True.*
6. *False.* Expanding open interest in a downtrend represents aggressive new short selling and is bearish.

ADVANCED ANALYSIS

OSCILLATORS

Oscillators serve many purposes, but they are primarily designed to give a clearer picture of market action. They are relatively easy to construct and interpret.

One of the virtues of oscillators is that they can be used regardless of whether prices are moving up, down, or sideways. Many other technical tools have diminished value when prices are moving sideways.

This lesson will examine the three main types of oscillators and the methods used to interpret each.

Oscillator Interpretation

Oscillators are typically constructed with lower and upper boundaries, such as -1 to $+1$ or 0 to 100. Oscillator readings range between the lower and upper boundaries. Typically, peaks and lows in the oscillator correspond to peaks and lows in market prices.

Before describing the three main types of oscillators, let's examine three common methods of interpreting oscillators.

Crossing of the Midpoint Line   When the oscillator crosses the midpoint line, a signal is given that prices will move in the direction of the crossing. If the oscillator moves up through the midpoint line, it is bullish. On the other hand, if the oscillator declines through the midpoint line, it is considered to be a bearish sign for prices.

The midpoint line is typically zero for oscillators that range from negative to positive numbers (i.e., −1 to +1). For oscillators with lower and upper boundaries of 0 and 100, the midpoint line is 50.

TECHNICAL ANALYSIS TIP

The saying "Don't fight the trend!" is frequently heard on Wall Street. Keep in mind that you will have a greater probability of success when you follow oscillator signals from midpoint line crossovers if they are in the direction of the prevailing trend in prices.

Divergence Analysis   When market prices make a high, correct, and then make a new high, and at the same time, the oscillator makes a high, corrects, and then does not make a new high, a bearish divergence occurs. That suggests that market prices are likely to go lower.

Similarly, when market prices make a low, correct, and then make a new low, and the oscillator makes a corresponding low, corrects, and then does not reach a new low, a bullish divergence occurs. The implication of a bullish divergence is that market prices are likely to rise.

Extreme Readings   Extreme high readings suggest an overbought condition and are, therefore, viewed as bearish. Extreme low readings are interpreted as prices reaching an oversold condition that is bullish. Note that oscillators can remain at extreme readings for lengthy periods of time. Thus, it is best to recognize extreme readings as periods of market vulnerability and not as specific buy and sell signals.

Types of Oscillators

There are three main types of oscillators:

1. Momentum oscillators.
2. Rate of change oscillators.
3. Moving average oscillators.

Each type will be described in detail in the following sections.

MOMENTUM OSCILLATORS

Momentum measures the acceleration or deceleration of prices rather than actual price levels. A *momentum oscillator* is constructed to measure that speed or rate of change.

To create a momentum oscillator, subtract the closing period's price for a certain number of periods ago from the current period's closing price. Do this each period and plot the amounts calculated. For example, a five-day momentum oscillator is the difference between the current day's closing price and the closing price five days ago. Each day this positive or negative value is plotted around the zero line as illustrated in Figure 12-1 for the Standard & Poor's 500 Index.

The following table shows how the momentum oscillator reacts based on the price gains for the current period's activity versus those for N periods ago. Note that N can be any number of periods one chooses.

Momentum Oscillator	Description
Up	Prices rose by more (or declined by less) in the current period than N periods ago.
Flat	Prices rose or declined by an equal amount in the current period than N periods ago.
Down	Prices rose by less (or declined by more) in the current period than N periods ago.

One of the benefits of the momentum oscillator is that it leads price action at market turning points. It then flattens out while the current price trend is in effect.

RATE OF CHANGE OSCILLATORS

Rate of change oscillators are simply momentum oscillators in percentage rather than point change form. They are constructed as the ratio of the current closing price to the price a certain number of periods ago. For example, a five-day rate of change oscillator is calculated by dividing the current day's closing price by the closing price five days ago. Often the calculated rate of change value is multiplied by 100 and shown in percentage terms. In such a case, the oscillator will fluctuate above and below the 100 level.

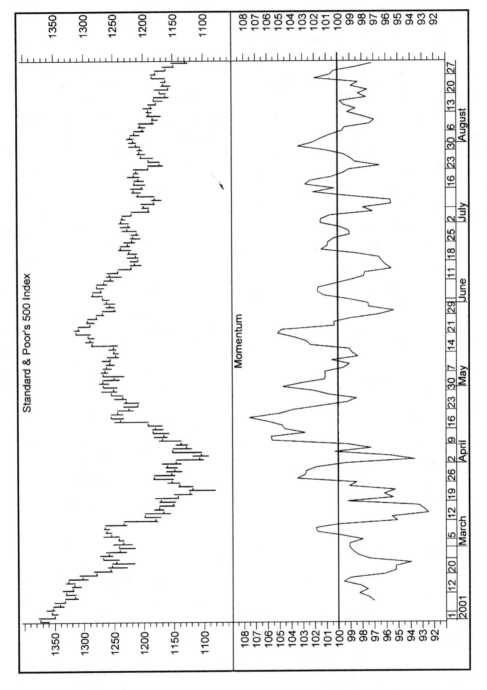

Figure 12-1 Standard & Poor's 500 Index (*top*) versus Five-Day Momentum Oscillator (*bottom*)

Figure 12-2 illustrates a five-day rate of change oscillator for the Standard & Poor's 500 Index.

MOVING AVERAGE OSCILLATORS

A *moving average oscillator* is constructed by taking the difference between two moving averages of different lengths and plotting that difference. The difference can be the point difference or percentage difference between the two moving averages.

The purposes of constructing a moving average oscillator are to:

1. Identify divergences.
2. Note significant deviations caused by the shorter-term moving average moving far away from the longer-term moving average.
3. To make moving average crossovers easy to see. When the oscillator crosses the zero line, the two moving averages have crossed each other.

Let's look at an example. Figure 12-3 shows an oscillator based on 10- and 50-day simple moving averages of the Standard & Poor's 500 Index. Note that when the 10-day moving average is above the 50-day moving average, the oscillator is at a positive value. On the other hand, when the 10-day moving average is below the 50-day moving average, the oscillator reading is negative.

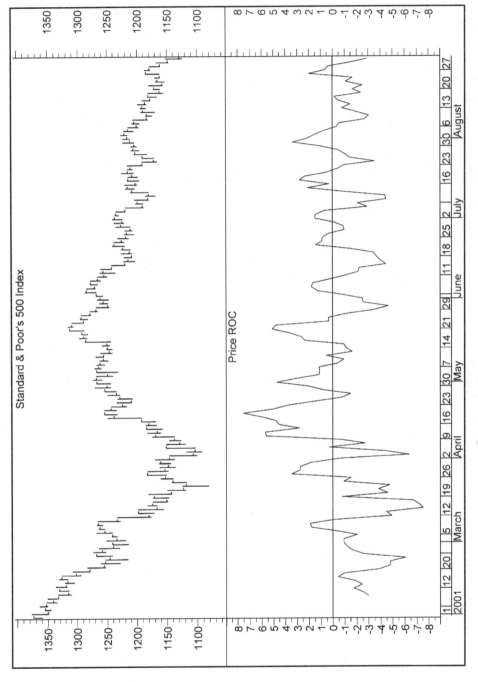

Figure 12-2 Standard & Poor's 500 Index (*top*) versus Five-Day Rate of Change Oscillator (*bottom*)

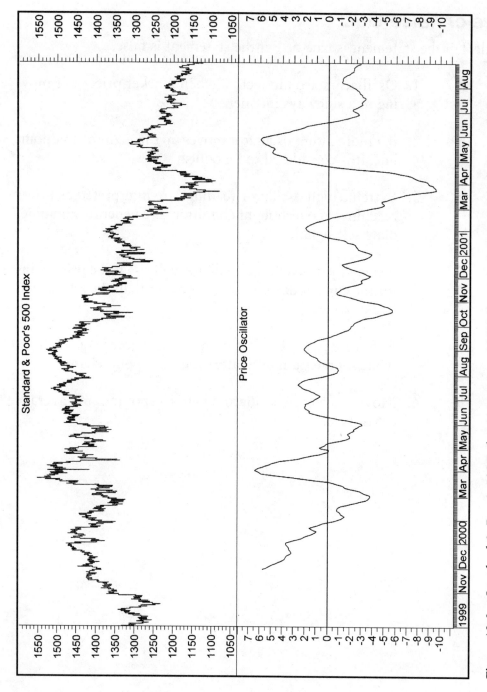

Figure 12-3   Standard & Poor's 500 Index (*top*) versus 10/50-Day Moving Average Oscillator (*bottom*)

165

True or False Quiz

Circle **T** if the statement is true or **F** if the statement is false.

T   F   1. Oscillators are ineffective when market prices are moving in a sideways manner.

T   F   2. If a momentum oscillator moves up through the midpoint line, it is considered to be bullish.

T   F   3. Extreme high oscillator readings are interpreted as prices reaching an overbought condition and generate an immediate sell signal.

T   F   4. A five-day momentum oscillator will rise if the price gains for the current day's activity is greater than the advance of five days ago.

T   F   5. Rate-of-change oscillators measure percentage change, while momentum oscillators measure point change.

T   F   6. Moving average oscillators help to spot moving average crossovers.

Answers

1. *False.* Oscillators can be beneficial regardless of whether prices are moving up, down, or sideways.
2. *True.*
3. *False.* Oscillators can remain at extreme readings for lengthy periods of time. Therefore, extreme readings should be viewed as periods of market vulnerability and not as specific buy and sell signals.
4. *True.*
5. *True.*
6. *True.* When a moving average oscillator crosses the midpoint line, the two moving averages have crossed each other.

RELATIVE STRENGTH INDEX

The *Relative Strength Index* (RSI) is a price momentum indicator developed by J. Welles Wilder, Jr. Since its introduction in Wilder's 1978 book *New Concepts In Technical Trading Systems*, it has become widely used by technicians, particularly those who are commodities and futures oriented.

RSI is frequently confused with relative strength analysis, which compares the performance of two items (such as, one stock with another or one stock with an overall market index). Its name is the only thing it has in common with relative strength analysis.

Conceptual Basis of the Relative Strength Index

Lesson 12 discussed rate of change oscillators. RSI is a rate of change oscillator. It measures the velocity at which prices are moving.

RSI was intentionally designed to address three flaws often associated with oscillators. First, at times, oscillators move erratically due to the drop off of old data in their calculation. For example, if one has a 10-day oscillator and 10 days ago the price of the security moved up or down dramatically, the current oscillator reading will be a misleading low or high reading. A second problem relates to the vertical scale for an oscillator. How high or low should the oscillator be to signal buying or selling opportunities? The third and final problem is the need to keep massive amounts of data for oscillator calculations. RSI presents a solution to these problems.

How to Calculate the Relative Strength Index

RSI is calculated as follows:

$$RSI = 100 - \frac{100}{1 + RS}$$

$$RS = \frac{\text{Average of N period's up closes}}{\text{Average of N period's down closes}}$$

N = number of periods used in the calculation

Let's use 14 days as an example. To get the average up value, add the total points gained on up days during the last 14 days and divide by 14. The average down value is arrived at by adding the total points lost on down days during the last 14 days and dividing by 14. Divide the average up value by the average down value to calculate RS. Insert the RS value into the formula and calculate the first day's RSI value.

Updating RSI each period is easy. Simply multiply the previous up and down average values by 13, add the latest day's gain or loss to the up or down average, and multiply the total by 14. Insert the new RS value into the RSI formula and recalculate RSI.

Table 13-1 shows a complete example of calculating RSI for 14 days. Wilder suggests the use of 14 days of data in the RSI calculation; however, other technicians have found that other time periods work with success as well.

In general, the greater the number of periods used, the more stable RSI is, and the fewer signals are generated. Short-term RSIs tend to produce more signals than longer-term RSIs, including more false signals.

Figure 13-1 compares RSIs of differing lengths—9 and 14 days—for the Standard & Poor's 500 Index. Note the difference in the number of crossings of the 70 and 30 lines.

Interpreting the Relative Strength Index

RSI can be interpreted from the following five perspectives:

1. Extreme readings.
2. Chart patterns.

Table 13-1 Example of How to Calculate the Relative Strength Index

Day	Closing Price	Change in Price from Prior Day Up	Change in Price from Prior Day Down	Totals for Last 14 Days Up (A)	Totals for Last 14 Days Down (B)	Averages for Last 14 Days Up (A)/14 = (C)	Averages for Last 14 Days Down (B)/14 = (D)	Up Average Divided by Down Average (C)/(D) = (E)	1 + (E) = (F)	100/(F) = (G)	RSI -100(G)
1	43.000										
2	44.125	1.125									
3	43.250		0.875								
4	42.875		0.375								
5	43.000	0.125									
6	42.875		0.125								
7	42.625		0.250								
8	42.125		0.500								
9	42.750	0.625									
10	43.750	1.000									
11	44.125	0.375									
12	43.750		0.375								
13	44.500	0.750									
14	44.125		0.375	4.000	2.875	0.286	0.205	1.391	2.391	41.818	58.182
15	44.125			4.000	2.875	0.286	0.205	1.391	2.391	41.818	58.182
16	44.875	0.750		3.625	2.875	0.259	0.205	1.261	2.261	44.231	55.769
17	45.000	0.125		3.750	2.000	0.268	0.143	1.875	2.875	34.783	65.217
18	44.375		0.625	3.750	2.250	0.268	0.161	1.667	2.667	37.500	62.500
19	43.875		0.500	3.625	2.750	0.259	0.196	1.318	2.318	43.137	56.863
20	42.750		1.125	3.625	3.750	0.259	0.268	0.967	1.967	50.847	49.153
21	42.625		0.125	3.625	3.625	0.259	0.259	1.000	2.000	50.000	50.000
22	44.000	1.375		5.000	3.125	0.357	0.223	1.600	2.600	38.462	61.538
23	43.750		0.250	4.375	3.375	0.313	0.241	1.296	2.296	43.548	56.452
24	43.375		0.375	3.375	3.750	0.241	0.268	0.900	1.900	52.632	47.368
25	42.875		0.500	3.000	4.250	0.214	0.304	0.706	1.706	58.621	41.379
26	43.625	0.750		3.750	3.875	0.268	0.277	0.968	1.968	50.820	49.180
27	44.750	1.125		4.125	3.875	0.295	0.277	1.065	2.065	48.438	51.563
28	43.750		1.000	4.125	4.500	0.295	0.321	0.917	1.917	52.174	47.826
29	43.625		0.125	4.125	4.625	0.295	0.330	0.892	1.892	52.857	47.143

Table 13-1 Example of How to Calculate the Relative Strength Index (*Continued*)

Day	Closing Price	Change in Price from Prior Day Up	Down	Totals for Last 14 Days Up (A)	Down (B)	Averages for Last 14 Days Up (A)/14 = (C)	Down (B)/14 = (D)	Up Average Divided by Down Average (C)/(D) = (E)	1 + (E) = (F)	100/(F) = (G)	RSI −100(G)
30	43.125		0.500	3.375	5.125	0.241	0.366	0.659	1.659	60.294	39.706
31	43.625	0.500		3.750	5.125	0.268	0.366	0.732	1.732	57.746	42.254
32	43.625			3.750	4.500	0.268	0.321	0.833	1.833	54.545	45.455
33	43.375		0.250	3.750	4.250	0.268	0.304	0.882	1.882	53.125	46.875
34	43.875	0.500		4.250	3.125	0.304	0.223	1.360	2.360	42.373	57.627
35	45.000	1.125		5.375	3.000	0.384	0.214	1.792	2.792	35.821	64.179
36	45.375	0.375		4.375	3.000	0.313	0.214	1.458	2.458	40.678	59.322
37	45.375			4.375	2.750	0.313	0.196	1.591	2.591	38.596	61.404
38	45.500	0.125		4.500	2.375	0.321	0.170	1.895	2.895	34.545	65.455
39	45.000		0.500	4.500	2.375	0.321	0.170	1.895	2.895	34.545	65.455
40	43.625		1.375	3.750	3.750	0.268	0.268	1.000	2.000	50.000	50.000
41	43.375		0.250	2.625	4.000	0.188	0.286	0.656	1.656	60.377	39.623
42	43.125		0.250	2.625	3.250	0.188	0.232	0.808	1.808	55.319	44.681
43	43.125			2.625	3.125	0.188	0.223	0.840	1.840	54.348	45.652
44	44.250	1.125		3.750	2.625	0.268	0.188	1.429	2.429	41.176	58.824
45	43.500		0.750	3.250	3.375	0.232	0.241	0.963	1.963	50.943	49.057
46	44.375	0.875		4.125	3.375	0.295	0.241	1.222	2.222	45.000	55.000
47	45.875	1.500		5.625	3.125	0.402	0.223	1.800	2.800	35.714	64.286
48	46.750	0.875		6.000	3.125	0.429	0.223	1.920	2.920	34.247	65.753
49	47.625	0.875		5.750	3.125	0.411	0.223	1.840	2.840	35.211	64.789
50	48.000	0.375		5.750	3.125	0.411	0.223	1.840	2.840	35.211	64.789

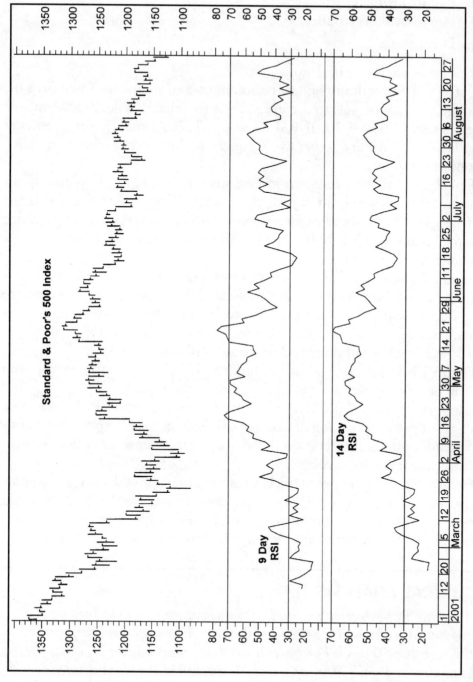

Figure 13-1   Comparison of Standard & Poor's 500 Index (*top*), 9-Day Relative Strength Index (*middle*), and 14-Day Relative Strength Index (*bottom*)

173

3. Failure swings.
4. Support and resistance.
5. Divergence.

Let's examine each one in detail.

Extreme RSI readings signal the likelihood of major tops or bottoms. Although the exact levels to use are subject to debate, Wilder recommends using levels of 70 and 30. If RSI rises above 70, a major top in market prices is likely. A decline to below 30 suggests a high probability of a major bottom being made.

The chart patterns presented in Lessons 3 through 5 are equally applicable to RSI as they are to regular price charts. Often, chart patterns (such as a triangle or head and shoulders top or bottom) can be seen in RSI. Since the same breakout rules apply to RSI as to normal price charts, buy and sell points are frequently indicated.

Failure swings can also be used in interpretation of RSI. First of all, let's define what a failure swing is. As illustrated in Figure 13-2, a top failure swing occurs when the index rises above 70, declines to a lower level (fail point), rises again failing to reach the 70 level, and then falls below the prior lower level (a fail point). One would sell at that point.

Figure 13-3 illustrates a bottom failure swing. It is simply the opposite of a top failure swing.

Support and resistance lines will often be apparent on RSI before the bar chart of prices. Breaking of support or resistance is interpreted in a similar fashion to the interpretation of price charts. Refer to Lesson 7 on support and resistance for a refresher.

Finally, divergence between prices on a bar chart and RSI strongly suggests that prices will be reversing. If prices are rising or flat and RSI is decreasing, look for a turn downward in prices. If, on the other hand, prices are declining or flat and RSI is increasing, expect prices to turn and move higher.

TECHNICAL ANALYSIS TIP

A simple but effective method of interpreting RSI is to buy on the crossing up through the 50 level and sell on the crossing down through the 50 level. For overall stock market indexes (such as the Standard & Poor's 500 Index), a 21-week RSI is recommended.

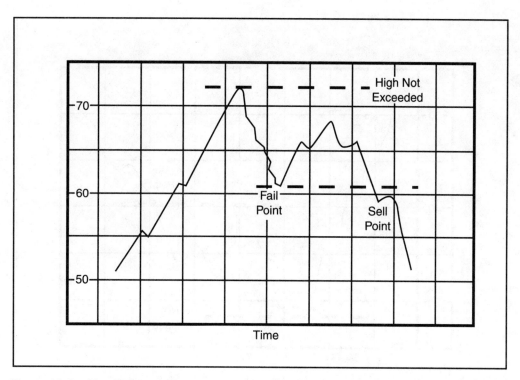

Figure 13-2   Top Failure Swing

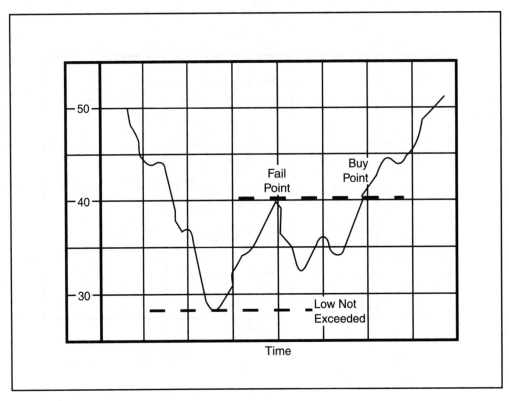

Figure 13-3   Bottom Failure Swing

True or False Quiz

Circle T if the statement is true or F if the statement is false.

T   F   1. RSI is a rate of change oscillator.

T   F   2. Wilder suggests that when RSI rises above 70, it is bullish.

T   F   3. Chart patterns that appear on RSI charts should be interpreted in a similar manner to those appearing on bar charts.

T   F   4. Support and resistance lines will often become apparent on RSI before the bar chart of prices.

Answers

1. *True.*
2. *False.* If RSI rises above 70, a major top in market prices is likely. Therefore, it should be viewed as bearish.
3. *True.*
4. *True.*

STOCHASTICS

The stochastics approach to market analysis was developed by George C. Lane (Investment Educators). It has become very popular among investors, especially those who are short-term oriented (although it is equally effective for longer investment horizons).

Stochastics is a price velocity technique based on the theory that as prices increase, closing prices have a tendency to be ever nearer to the highs for the period. Similarly, as prices move lower, closing prices tend to be closer and closer to the lows for the period.

Calculation

The formula for calculating stochastics is as follows:

$$\%K = \frac{(C - L)}{(H - L)} \times 100$$

where:

$\%K$ is stochastics.

C   is the latest closing price.

L   is the low price during the last N periods.

H   is the high price during the last N periods.

N   can be any number of periods

    (Lane recommends using from 5 to 21 periods).

%K is then smoothed, typically using a three-period simple moving average, to derive %D.

The resulting %K and %D lines when plotted show, on a percentage basis of 0 to 100, where the closing price is relative to the range of prices for a given period of time (i.e., five days).

An example of stochastics is provided in Figure 14-1. The upper half of the chart is a bar chart of the Standard & Poor's 500 Index. The bottom half is the stochastics plot.

Divergence Analysis

The principal method of interpreting stochastics for buy and sell signals is through divergence analysis. A bearish divergence (see Figure 14-2) occurs when a security's price makes a high, then corrects moving lower, and subsequently reaches a higher high. At the same time, corresponding peaks of the %D line make a high followed by a lower high. Confirmation and the signal to sell occurs when the %K line moves below the %D line.

A bullish divergence (see Figure 14-3) occurs when a security's price makes a low, then corrects moving higher, and subsequently reaches a lower low. At the same time, corresponding bottoms of the %D line make a low followed by a higher low. Confirmation and the signal to buy comes when the %K line moves above the %D line.

TECHNICAL ANALYSIS TIP

Signals to buy and sell have a higher probability of success if they are given in the 10 percent to 15 percent range for buy signals (bullish divergences) and the 85 percent to 90 percent range for sell signals (bearish divergences).

Extreme Readings

It is not unusual for the %K line to reach 0 or 100 percent. These readings do not mean that the price of a particular security has reached a bottom (0 percent) or top (100 percent). It does suggest great weakness (0 percent) or strength (100 percent).

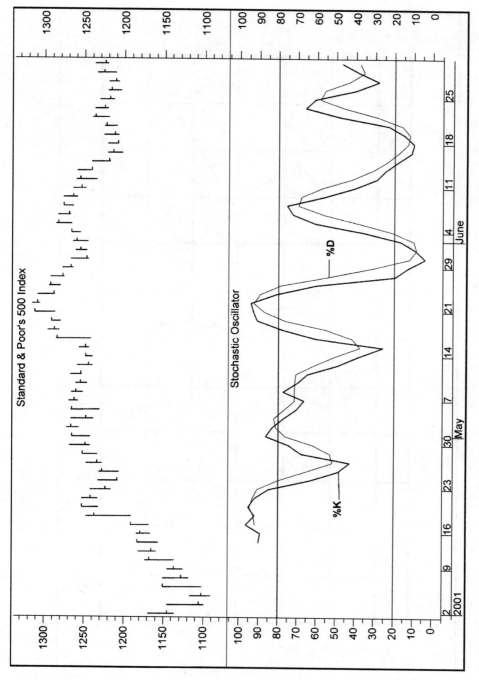

Figure 14-1 Standard & Poor's 500 Index (*top*) versus Five-Day Stochastics Plot (*bottom*)

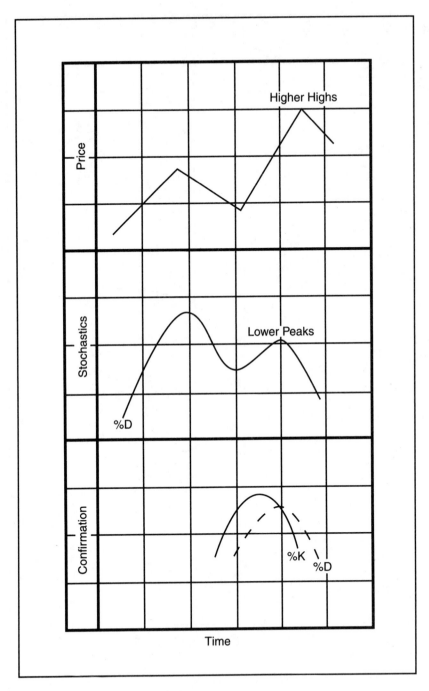

Figure 14-2   Example of a Bearish Divergence

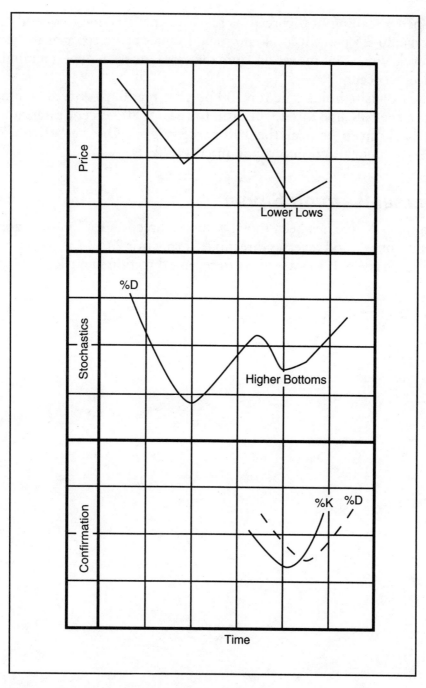

Figure 14-3 Example of a Bullish Divergence

When a reading of 0 percent is reached, the %K line frequently moves up to the 20–25 percent level and then declines again to or near the 0 percent level. When %K moves up from that area, one can expect a minor rally in prices to occur.

The opposite holds true for 100 percent readings. After reaching 100 percent, the %K line often will drop to the 75–80 percent range and then move back up to or near the 100 percent level. On the %K line's next decline, a minor reaction (drop in prices) is likely.

Reversal Warning Signal

When the %K line has been moving in one direction for many periods and suddenly, one period reverses direction sharply (for 2 to 12 percent), a warning signal is given. Prices are likely to reverse direction in one or two periods.

True or False Quiz

Circle **T** if the statement is true or **F** if the statement is false.

T   F   1. The stochastics approach is only effective for short-term analysis.

T   F   2. Stochastics is based on the theory that as prices increase (or decrease), closing prices have a tendency to be closer and closer to the highs (or lows) for the period.

T   F   3. Divergence analysis is the principal method of using stochastics to generate buy and sell signals.

T   F   4. A %K line reading of 0 percent means that the price of a security has reached a bottom.

Answers

1. *False.* The stochastics approach is equally as effective for long-term analysis as it is for the short-term.
2. *True.*
3. *True.*
4. *False.* A %K line reading of 0 percent implies great weakness, not that the price of a security has reached a bottom.

MOVING AVERAGE CONVERGENCE-DIVERGENCE

Moving Average Convergence-Divergence (MACD) is a price momentum indicator that was developed by Gerald Appel (Signalert Corporation). It is an oscillator based on the point spread difference between two exponential moving averages of the closing price—a slower one (typically 26-period) and a faster one (typically 12-period). This difference is further smoothed by an even faster exponential moving average (typically 9-period) which is called the signal line.

An example of MACD is provided in Figure 15-1. The upper half of the chart is a bar chart of the Standard & Poor's 500 Index. The bottom half is the MACD plot including the signal line.

Although 26- and 12-period exponential moving averages are typically used for MACD and a 9-period exponential moving average is normally used for the signal line calculation, other exponential moving averages can be used. There is no set number of exponential moving average periods that work best in all markets and for all investment time horizons. Only by experimenting with the particular security or market you are trading can you determine the best combination of exponential moving average periods to use in the MACD calculation.

MACD can be viewed from three perspectives, namely, divergence analysis, extreme readings, and crossover of MACD by the signal line.

Divergence Analysis

The primary method of interpreting MACD for buy and sell signals is through divergence analysis. Divergence between prices on a bar chart and

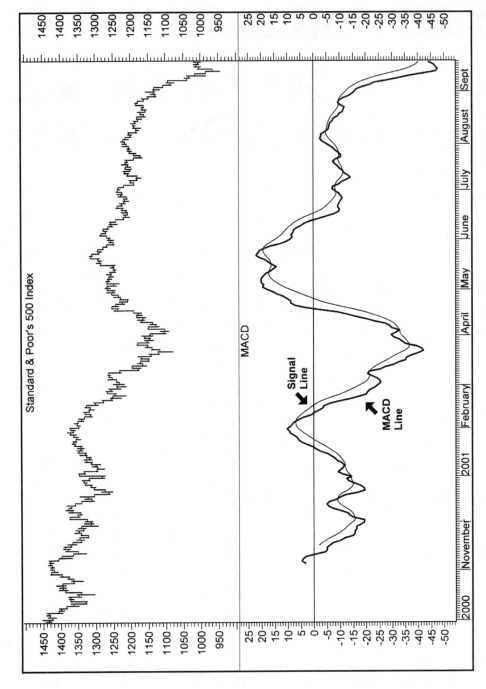

Figure 15-1   Standard & Poor's 500 Index (*top*) versus Moving Average Convergence-Divergence (*bottom*).

MACD strongly suggests that prices will be reversing direction. If prices are rising or moving sideways and MACD is declining, look for a downturn in prices. If, on the other hand, prices are declining or moving sideways and MACD is increasing, expect prices to turn and move higher.

Extreme Readings

As with many technical indicators, extreme MACD readings identify over-bought and oversold conditions, thereby signaling the likelihood of tops or bottoms. When MACD is extremely high, a top in prices is likely. Conversely, an extremely low MACD reading suggests a high probability of a bottom being made.

Crossover of MACD by the Signal Line

In general, when the MACD line crosses from below to above the signal line, it is considered bullish. On the other hand, it is viewed as bearish when the MACD line crosses from above to below the signal line. However, the crossover signal should not be used in isolation, but as confirmation of bullish and bearish evidence provided by examining MACD for divergences from price action and extreme readings.

TECHNICAL ANALYSIS TIP

A warning! Do not turn MACD into a mechanical system whereby you buy when the MACD line crosses above the signal line and sell when the MACD line crosses below the signal line. MACD was not designed or intended to be used in that fashion. If you treat MACD as a mechanical system, it is likely that you will be very disappointed with the results and will lose money.

True or False Quiz

Circle T if the statement is true or F if the statement is false.

T   F   1. In calculating MACD, there is no set number of exponential moving average periods that work best in all markets and for all investment time horizons.

T   F   2. Crossover of MACD by the signal line is the principal method of using MACD to generate buy and sell signals.

T   F   3. An extremely low MACD reading suggests a high probability of a top in prices being made.

Answers

1. *True.*
2. *False.* Divergence analysis is the principal method of using MACD to generate buy and sell signals.
3. *False.* An extremely low MACD reading suggests a high probability of a bottom in prices being made.

BOLLINGER BANDS

The technique of Bollinger Bands was developed by John Bollinger (Capital Growth Letter) to factor in price volatility. Bollinger Bands are effective for virtually any security or market and for any investment time horizon.

Rather than placing bands at a certain percentage distance from a moving average line as is done with envelopes (also known as trading bands—see Figure 16-1 for an example), Bollinger Bands are placed two moving standard deviations above and below a simple moving average line. More specifically, the bands are placed above and below a simple moving average at a distance of two times the root mean square of the deviations from the average. The amount of data used in the calculation is equal to the number of periods used for the simple moving average. For example, if you use a 20-day simple moving average, all calculations should be based on 20 days of data.

TECHNICAL ANALYSIS TIP

Given the complexity of the calculations involved, do not attempt to use Bollinger Bands without the aid of a personal computer and technical analysis software or by accessing an Internet charting site. It is simply too time-consuming to perform this type of analysis by hand.

There is no set number of periods to use for the simple moving average or number of standard deviations above and below that work best in all

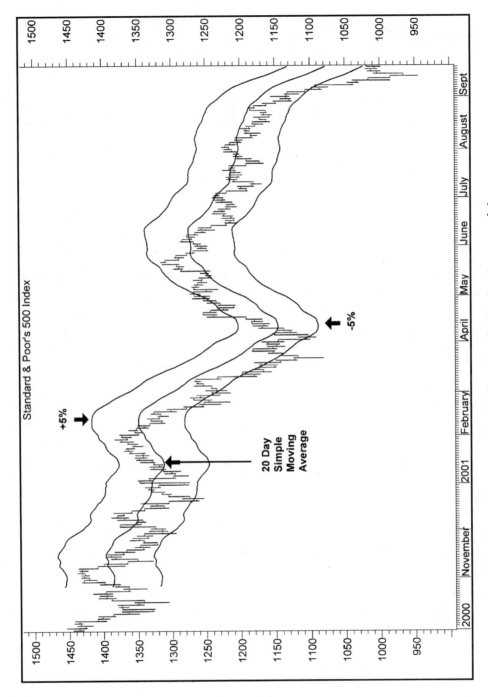

Figure 16-1　Five Percent Envelope around a 20-Day Simple Moving Average of the Standard & Poor's 500 Index

markets and for all investment time horizons. As with many technical indicators, only by experimenting with the particular security or market you are trading can you determine the best combination of simple moving average and standard deviations to use in plotting Bollinger Bands.

However, as a starting point, recommendation is made that you use a 10-period simple moving average with bands 1.5 moving standard deviations above and below for short-term analysis as illustrated in Figure 16-2. For intermediate-term analysis, a 20-period simple moving average with bands 2.0 moving standard deviations above and below can be used (see Figure 16-3 for an example). Long-term analysis can be accomplished with a 50-period moving average with bands 2.5 moving standard deviations above and below (see Figure 16-4 for an example).

Indicator Interpretation

Although calculating Bollinger Bands is complex, interpreting the indicator is fairly simple. Similar to normal trading bands, prices have a tendency to move from one Bollinger Band to the other. This gives you an opportunity to project price levels to be reached.

Again, as with normal trading bands, when prices close above the upper Bollinger Band, it is a sign of great market strength and a buying opportunity. Conversely, when prices close below the lower Bollinger Band, great market weakness is signaled.

When there is a decrease in market volatility, the upper and lower Bollinger Bands move closer to the simple moving average line. There is a tendency for sharp price moves after such occurrences.

Finally, when price bottoms form first above the upper Bollinger Band and then below it, a reversal in trend from down to up is signaled. Conversely, when tops develop first below the lower Bollinger Band and then above it, a trend reversal from up to down is signaled.

Figure 16-2 Standard & Poor's 500 Index with Short-Term Bollinger Bands (10-Day Simple Moving Average; 1.5 Standard Deviations)

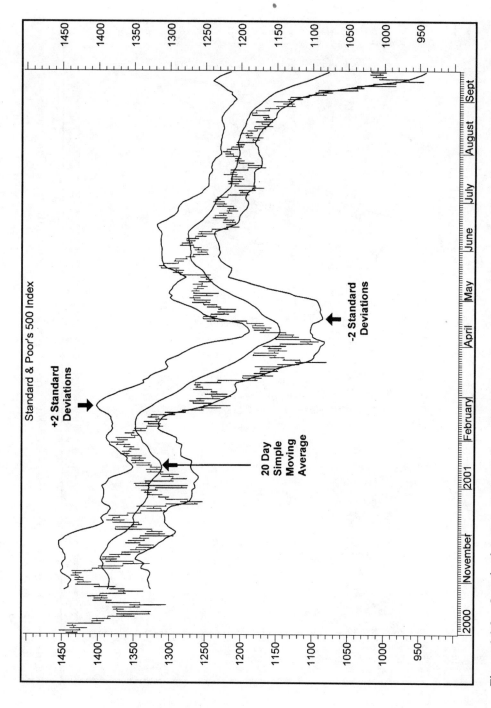

Figure 16-3   Standard & Poor's 500 Index with Intermediate-Term Bollinger Bands (20-Day Simple Moving
Average; 2.0 Standard Deviations)

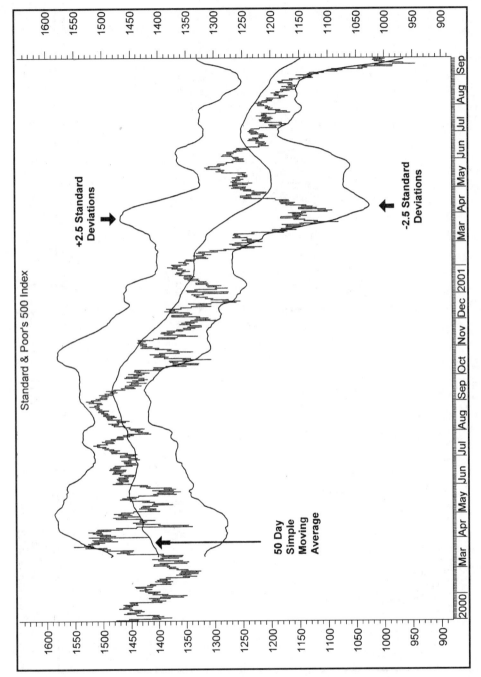

Figure 16-4   Standard & Poor's 500 Index with Long-Term Bollinger Bands (50-Day Moving Average; 2.5 Standard Deviations)

True or False Quiz

Circle **T** if the statement is true or **F** if the statement is false.

T   F   1. A 20-day simple moving average with bands 2.0 moving standard deviations above and below should always be used for intermediate-term analysis.

T   F   2. Prices have a tendency to move from one Bollinger Band to the other.

T   F   3. When prices move above the upper Bollinger Band, it is a sign of great market strength and a potential buying opportunity.

Answers

1. *False.* There is no set number of periods to use for the simple moving average or number of standard deviations above and below that work best for all securities and in all markets for intermediate-term analysis.
2. *True.*
3. *True.*

ALTERNATIVE CHARTING METHODS

POINT AND FIGURE CHARTING

Although not used as widely as bar charts, *point and figure charts* have been around since the late 1800s. This lesson will show how to construct and interpret point and figure charts.

Point and Figure Charts versus Bar Charts

Bar charts are by far the most popular type of charts used by technicians. In addition to bar charts, a significant number of technicians use point and figure charts to track market action.

What are the differences between point and figure charts and bar charts? There are two main ones.

First, visually the two types of charts look different. Figure 17-1 shows a daily point and figure chart of Fannie Mae for a one year period. Figure 17-2 provides a bar chart of Fannie Mae for the same time period.

By examining the horizontal axis on each chart, one notes that the time periods are evenly spaced out on the bar chart, but not on the point and figure chart. Point and figure charts are simply a study of price action. Time is not taken into consideration when prices are plotted.

A second difference relates to the recording of volume. Bar charts often include a volume histogram at the bottom of the chart (see Figure 17-2). Point and figure charts do not include a volume histogram or other graphic representation of volume activity. However, some technicians argue that volume is reflected in the number of price changes shown on the chart.

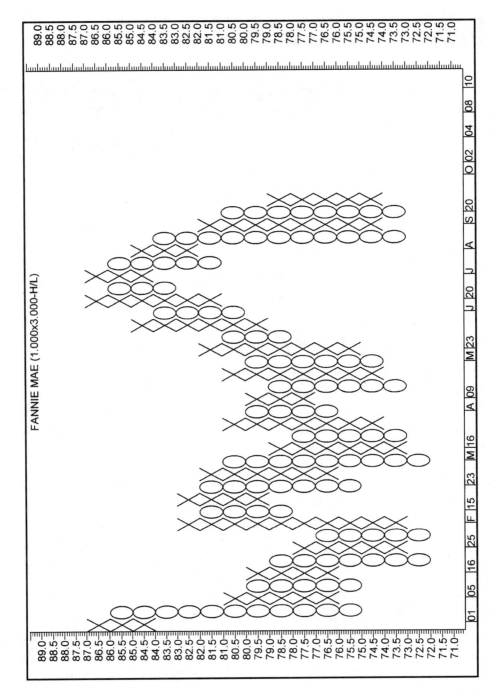

Figure 17-1   Point and Figure Chart for Fannie Mae

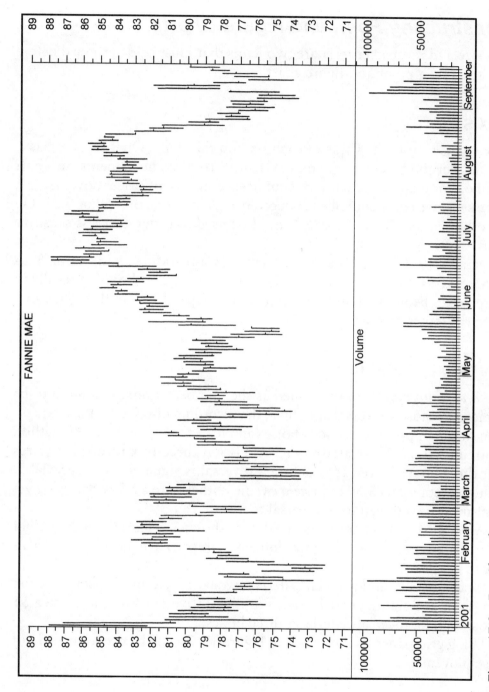

Figure 17-2   Bar Chart for Fannie Mae

Constructing Point and Figure Charts

Box size and reversal criteria are two items that must be determined before constructing a point and figure chart.

BOX SIZE

Box size is simply the value of each box on the chart. On a relative basis, the smaller the box size, the more sensitive to price movements the chart will be. For example, each box could represent $1 of price movement. A more sensitive chart could be produced using a box size of $.50 or $.25. On the other hand, a box size of $3 could be used to generate a less sensitive chart.

Figures 17-3 and 17-4 show the same data for McDonald's using $.25 and $.50 box sizes, respectively. Note that the smaller box size results in more boxes being used and a shorter-term perspective than that generated using the larger box size.

REVERSAL CRITERIA

The *reversal criteria* can be defined as the number of boxes required to be retraced to cause a reversal and, thus, the recording of prices in the next column in the opposite direction. For example, a three-box reversal method is often used. As illustrated in Figure 17-5, a three-box reversal requires that three boxes be retraced before a reversal is signaled. In Figure 17-5, each box represents $.50 of price movement; therefore $1.50 of price movement must be retraced for a reversal to occur.

A one-box reversal for the same data is shown in Figure 17-6. Note that reversals are more frequent, and longer-term price trends are more difficult to discern.

Once box size and reversal criteria have been determined, construction of a point and figure chart is easy. For illustrative purposes, let's use a $1 box size and a reversal criteria of three boxes.

Using grid paper, as illustrated in Figure 17-7, each box represents $1 of price movement.

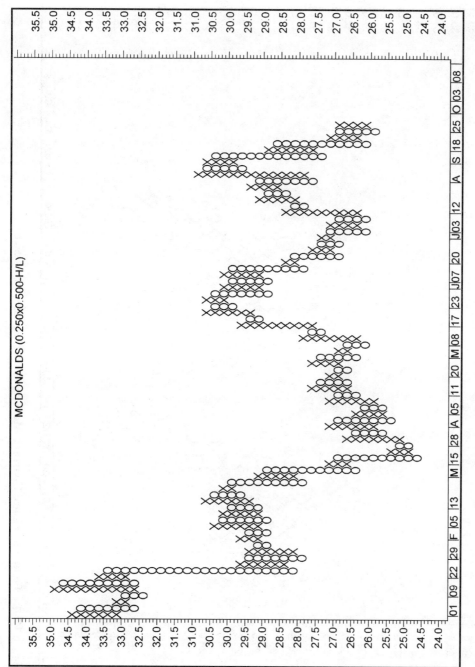

Figure 17-3   Point and Figure Chart for McDonald's Using a $.25 Box Size

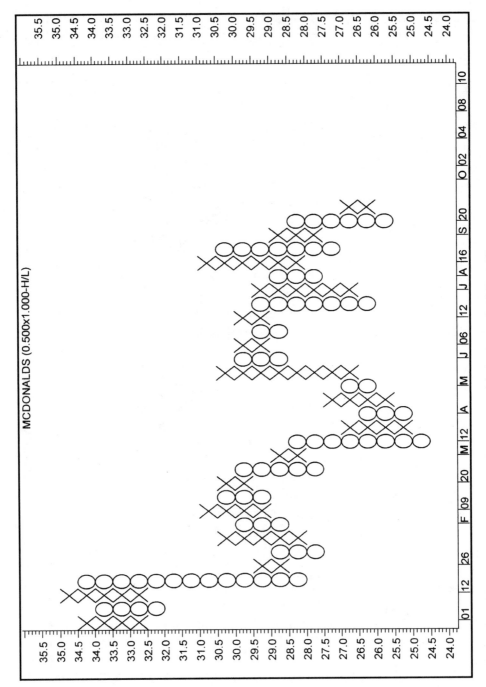

Figure 17-4   Point and Figure Chart for McDonald's Using a $.50 Box Size

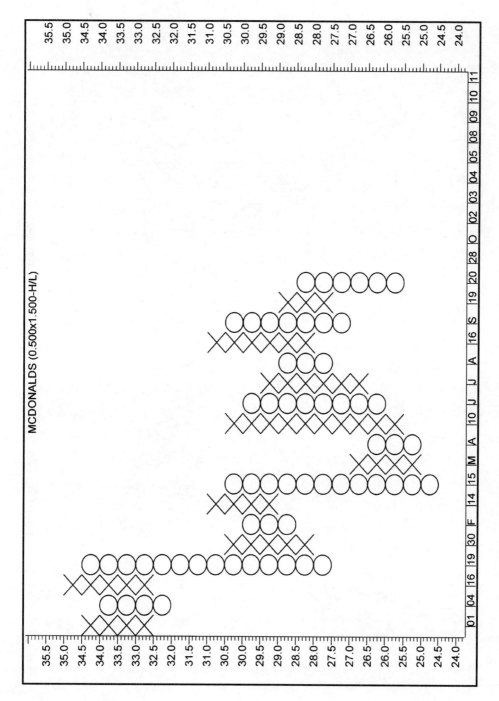

Figure 17-5   Point and Figure Chart for McDonald's Using a Three-Box Reversal

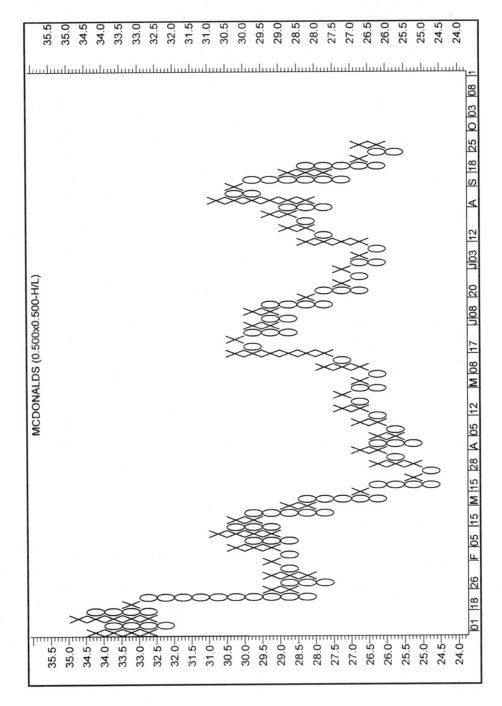

Figure 17-6 Point and Figure Chart for McDonald's Using a One-Box Reversal

Let's assume a stock trades at the following prices:

Period	Price
1	22
2	23
3	23.50
4	24
5	25
6	27
7	26
8	24
9	23

The first price, or X, representing up price movement, would be placed in the $22 box. Since prices moved up through $27, each box up through $27 would be filled with an X. During period 7, the price dropped from $27 to $26. However, since the reversal criterion is three boxes, nothing is plotted. The reversal criterion is met in period 8. Thus a 0 (representing down price movement) is placed in the $24 box in the next column. In the following period, the price dropped to $23, and another 0 is plotted.

TECHNICAL ANALYSIS TIP

Should you use intraday or daily price data? Pure point and figure chartists contend that point and figure charts should reflect all price activity occurring during the day and not just the closing price or low to high price range for the day. Some reversals will appear using intraday data that will not show on charts using low to high price range data. However, most investors have neither access to intraday, trade by trade data nor the time to plot it.

From a practical point of view the benefits of using intraday data are probably exceeded by the costs of obtaining and recording such information. It is suggested that you use the more readily available information, but recognize that from a pure point of view, all reversals may not be shown.

Chart Patterns

Just as with bar charts, chart patterns appear with enough frequency on point and figure charts to warrant watching for them. Head and shoulders and other chart patterns are similar to those associated with bar charts.

Trendlines

Trendlines can be drawn on point and figure charts just as they are drawn on bar charts. Up trendlines can be drawn by connecting lows, and down trendlines can be drawn by connecting highs. Interpretation of trendline breaks is the same as with bar charts.

Similarly, support and resistance lines, trend channel lines, and many other technical tools are equally valid on point and figure charts as they are on bar charts.

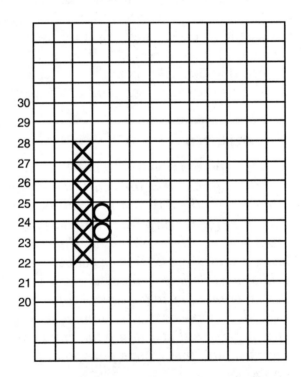

Figure 17-7   Example of Constructing a Point and Figure Chart with a $1 Box Size and Three-Box Reversal Criteria

True or False Quiz

Circle T if the statement is true or F if the statement is false.

T   F   1. Time periods are evenly spaced on the horizontal axis of both bar charts and point and figure charts.

T   F   2. The box size and reversal criteria must be determined before you can construct a point and figure chart.

T   F   3. The smaller the box size, the more sensitive to price movements the chart will be.

T   F   4. A head and shoulders top chart pattern on a point and figure chart should not be interpreted the same as a head and shoulders top chart pattern on a bar chart.

T   F   5. Trendlines, support and resistance lines, and many other technical tools are as valid on point and figure charts as they are on bar charts.

Answers

1. *False.* Time periods are evenly spaced out on bar charts but not on point and figure charts.
2. *True.*
3. *True.*
4. *False.* As with many chart patterns, interpretation of the head and shoulders top is the same on both a bar chart and a point and figure chart.
5. *True.*

JAPANESE CANDLESTICK CHARTING

Although candlestick charting has been used by Japanese traders for centuries, it has only recently captured the attention of Wall Street. This lesson will show you how to construct and interpret candlestick charts.

Before continuing, let's visually compare a candlestick chart to a bar chart. Figure 18-1 presents a standard bar chart. Figure 18-2 plots the same data in candlestick chart form. As can readily be seen, the two charting methods have many similarities. First, the scaling is the same. Second, the overall shape of the charts is the same. Third, both charts can be used in conjunction with other technical analysis tools (i.e., moving averages, oscillators, etc.). Fourth, the high-low range for each period is the same. Basically, the only difference is how the opening and closing prices are shown.

Constructing Candlestick Lines

Candlestick lines are easy to construct. Each line represents the trading activity for one period (i.e., hour, day, week, month, etc.) and shows opening, high, low, and closing prices.

The main body (the thick part) of the candlestick line represents the range between the period's opening and closing prices. If the closing price is higher than the opening price, the main body is white (empty). On the other hand, if the closing price is lower than the opening price, the main body is black (filled in).

The thin lines above and below the main body are called shadows. They show the high and low prices for the period (in a similar fashion to bar charts).

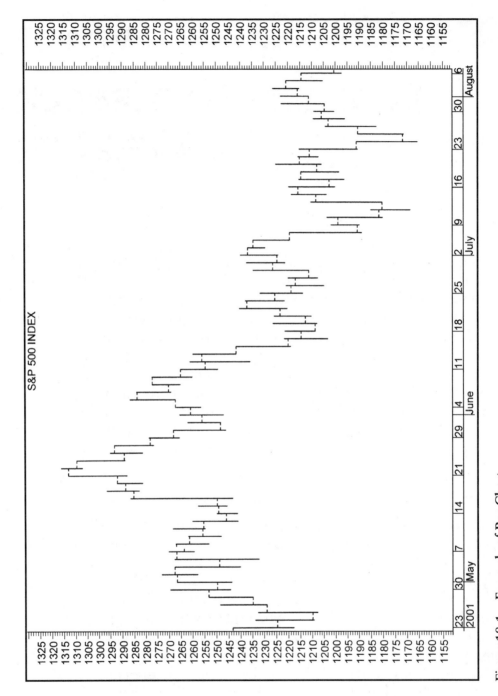

Figure 18-1   Example of Bar Chart

216

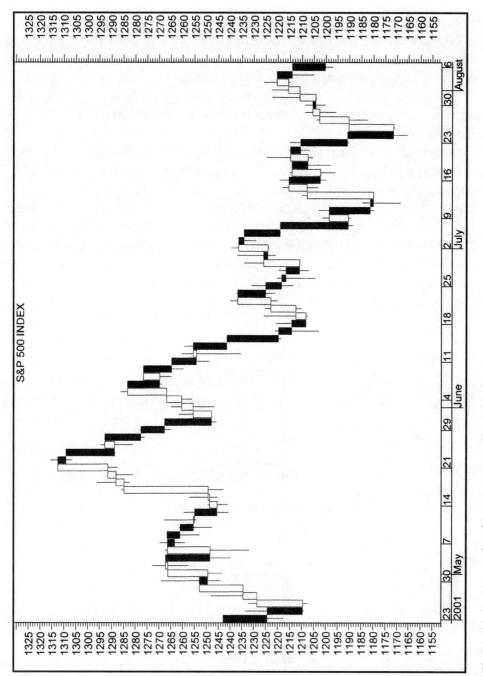

Figure 18-2   Example of Japanese Candlestick Chart

Figure 18-3 presents a long white body. This is considered bullish since prices closed near the high of the period after trading in a wide range.

Figure 18-4 illustrates a long black body. This is viewed as bearish since prices traded within a wide range and closed near the low of the period.

There can be periods in which the body is neither white nor black. This occurs when the opening and closing prices for a period are the same; it is known as a doji line.

Candlestick lines can take a variety of shapes depending upon the relationship of the period's opening, high, low, and closing prices. Figure 18-5 presents the more common shapes along with their interpretation.

As with bar charts, patterns can develop in candlestick charts that help forecast the future direction of prices. For purposes of discussion, we have divided the primary candlestick chart patterns into three types—bullish reversal, bearish reversal, and continuation.

Bullish reversal patterns are considered to be legitimate if formed after prices have been in a downtrend. Bearish reversal patterns appearing after an

Figure 18-3   Long White Body

Figure 18-4   Long Black Body

uptrend in prices are viewed as valid. Continuation patterns can occur in both upward and downward movements in prices.

Key Bullish Reversal Patterns

Hammer (see Figure 18-6): A hammer occurs when prices rally from an intraperiod sell-off to close near the open. This results in the main body, which can be either black or white, being at the upper end of the period's trading range with little or no upper shadow. The lower shadow must be at least twice the length of the main body for the pattern to be considered legitimate.

Bullish Engulfing Pattern (see Figure 18-7): A bullish engulfing pattern occurs when prices open lower than the previous period's close and then rally to close above the previous period's open. Thus, the current period's white main body engulfs the prior period's black main body. You should note that only the main body is important in this pattern; both upper and lower shadows are ignored.

Tweezer Bottom (see Figure 18-8): A tweezer bottom pattern is simply two consecutive periods with matching lows. It isn't important whether

Interpretation

1. Extremely bearish
2. Extremely bullish
3. Bearish
4. Bearish
5. Bullish
6. Bullish
7. Neutral
8. Neutral
9. In downtrend, bullish; in uptrend, bearish
10. In downtrend, bullish; in uptrend, bearish
11. A turning period
12. A turning period
13. End of downtrend
14. A turning period
15. Possible turning period

Figure 18-5   Various Candlestick Lines

Figure 18-6   Hammer

Figure 18-7   Bullish Engulfing Pattern

Figure 18-8   Tweezer Bottom

the candle lines have white or black main bodies (or are simply doji lines). There are no requirements regarding the length of upper and lower shadow lines. All that matters is that the lows for the two periods are the same.

Piercing Line (see Figure 18-9): A piercing line pattern occurs when prices gap lower on the opening and then retrace to close above the midpoint of the previous period's black body. This results in a period having a black main body being followed by a period with a white main body and, in the second period, (1) the open is lower than the previous period's low and (2) the close is higher than the center of the previous period's black main body.

Morning Star (see Figure 18-10): A morning star pattern develops over three periods. In the first period, prices close lower than they opened resulting in a black main body. In the second period, prices open lower creating a downside gap and close higher after trading in a relatively narrow range (a small main body). Finally, in the third period, prices continue to move higher and close above the midpoint of the first period's black main body.

Figure 18-9   Piercing Line

Figure 18-10   Morning Star

Bullish Doji Star (see Figure 18-11): A bullish doji star pattern occurs when prices gap to the downside on the open and then close at the same price as the open.

Bullish Harami (see Figure 18-12): A harami pattern is similar to an inside period. The open to close range (main body) for the current period falls within the open to close range (main body) of the previous period. Note that it doesn't matter whether the main bodies for the two periods are both black, both white, or one is black and one is white. What is important is when the pattern occurs. If a harami pattern occurs in a downtrend, it is considered a bullish reversal signal.

Bullish Harami Cross (see Figure 18-13): The harami cross pattern is the same as the harami chart formation except that the open and close are the same in the second period. If a harami cross pattern occurs in a downtrend, it is viewed as a bullish reversal signal.

Bullish Meeting Lines (see Figure 18-14): A bullish meeting lines pattern occurs when prices gap lower on the open and close unchanged from the previous period. A black main body in the first period is followed by a white main body in the second period.

Key Bearish Reversal Patterns

Hanging Man (see Figure 18-15): A hanging man occurs when prices rally from an intraperiod sell-off to close near the open. This results in the main

Figure 18-11   Bullish Doji Star

Figure 18-12   Bullish Harami

Figure 18-13   Bullish Harami Cross

Figure 18-14   Bullish Meeting Lines

Figure 18-15   Hanging Man

body, which can be either black or white, being at the upper end of the period's trading range with little or no upper shadow. The lower shadow must be at least twice the length of the main body for the pattern to be considered legitimate. Note that the only difference between a hanging man and a hammer is when the pattern occurs on the chart. If it develops after an uptrend in prices, it is a hanging man. If it forms after a downtrend in prices, it is a hammer. Regardless of whether you call the pattern a hanging man or a hammer, it signals a reversal in the trend of prices.

Bearish Engulfing Pattern (see Figure 18-16): A bearish engulfing pattern occurs when prices open higher than the previous period's close and then sell-off to close below the previous period's open. Thus, the current period's black main body engulfs the prior period's white main body. You should note that only the main body is important in this pattern; both upper and lower shadows are ignored.

Tweezer Top (see Figure 18-17): A tweezer top pattern is simply consecutive periods with matching highs. It isn't important whether the candle lines have white or black main bodies (or are simply doji lines). There are no requirements regarding the length of upper and lower shadow lines. All that matters is that the highs for the two periods are the same.

Dark Cloud Cover (see Figure 18-18): A dark cloud cover pattern occurs when prices gap higher on the opening and then retrace to close below the midpoint of the previous period's black body. This results in a period having a white main body being followed by a period with a black main body and, in the second period, (1) the open is higher than the previous period's

Figure 18-16   Bearish Engulfing Pattern

Figure 18-17   Tweezer Top

Figure 18-18   Dark Cloud Cover

high and (2) the close is lower than the center of the previous period's white main body.

Upside Gap Two Crows (see Figure 18-19): An upside gap two crows pattern forms when prices meet resistance on two consecutive days after gapping higher. A period having a white main body is followed by two periods with black main bodies. There is an upside gap between the white main body and the first black main body.

Evening Star (see Figure 18-20): An evening star pattern develops over three periods. In the first period, prices close higher than they open resulting in a white main body. In the second period, prices open higher creating an upside gap and close lower after trading in a relatively narrow range (a small main body). Finally, in the third period, prices continue to move lower and close below the midpoint of the first period's white main body.

Bearish Doji Star (see Figure 18-21): A bearish doji star pattern occurs when prices gap to the upside on the open and then close at the same price as the open.

Shooting Star (see Figure 18-22): A shooting star pattern is simply a period having a small main body, which can be either black or white, at the lower end of the price range with a long upper shadow.

Bearish Harami (see Figure 18-23): A harami pattern is similar to an inside period. The open to close range (main body) for the current period falls within the open to close range (main body) of the previous period. Note that it doesn't matter whether the main bodies for the two periods are both black, both white, or one is black and one is white. What is important is when the pattern occurs. If a harami pattern occurs in an uptrend, it is considered a bearish reversal signal.

Bearish Harami Cross (see Figure 18-24): The harami cross pattern is the same as the harami chart formation except that the open and close are the same in the second period. If a harami cross pattern occurs in an uptrend, it is viewed as a bearish reversal signal.

Figure 18-19   Upside Gap Two Crows

Figure 18-20   Evening Star

Figure 18-21   Bearish Doji Star

Figure 18-22   Shooting Star

Figure 18-23   Bearish Harami

Figure 18-24   Bearish Harami Cross

Figure 18-25   Bearish Meeting Lines

Bearish Meeting Lines (see Figure 18-25): A bearish meeting lines pattern occurs when prices gap higher on the open and then close unchanged from the previous period. A white main body in the first period is followed by a black main body in the second period.

Key Continuation Patterns

Window (see Figure 18-26): A window is simply a gap (an area on a chart where no actual trading takes place). Gaps frequently act as support or resistance. An upside window (gap) is considered to be bullish, while a downside window (gap) is viewed as bearish.

Upside Tasuki Gap (see Figure 18-27): An upside tasuki gap pattern develops over three periods. In the first period, prices close above their open resulting in a white main body. In the second period, prices gap to the upside on the open and then close higher (creating a white main body). In the third period, prices open within the main body of the second period and then close lower, but do not fill the gap (with either the main body or the lower shadow). This suggests that only a temporary setback has occurred and that prices will continue higher (in essence, because the gap has acted as a support level).

Rising Three Methods (see Figure 18-28): A rising three methods pattern occurs when a long white main body is followed by three or more small white or black main bodies and then a long white main body that makes a

Figure 18-26   Window

Figure 18-27   Upside Tasuki Gap

Figure 18-28   Rising Three Methods

new high close for the move. It is similar to a flag pattern on a bar chart and typically appears after a dynamic rally. It represents some profit-taking before the rally continues.

Falling Three Methods (see Figure 18-29): A falling three methods pattern occurs when a long black body is followed by three or more small white or black main bodies and then a long black main body that makes a new low close for the move. It is similar to a flag pattern on a bar chart and typically appears after a sharp downtrend. It represents short-covering before the drop in prices continues.

Side-by-Side White Lines (Upside Gap) (see Figure 18-30): This pattern develops over three periods. In the first period, the main body can be either white or black. Prices gap to the upside on the opening of the second period and then close higher. In the third period, prices open at the same opening price as in the second period and close higher. The inability of prices to fill the gap indicates a strong support level.

Side-by-Side White Lines (Downside Gap) (see Figure 18-31): This pattern develops over three periods. In the first period, the main body can be

Figure 18-29   Falling Three Methods

Figure 18-30   Side-by-Side White Lines (Upside Gap)

Figure 18-31   Side-by-Side White Lines (Downside Gap)

either white or black. Prices gap to the downside on the opening of the second period and then close higher. In the third period, prices close at the same closing price as in the second period after having risen from the open. The inability of prices to fill the gap indicates a strong resistance level.

True or False Quiz

Circle **T** if the statement is true or **F** if the statement is false.

T   F   1. The opening price, along with high, low, and closing prices for each period are required in order to prepare candlestick charts.

T   F   2. Candlestick charts more closely resemble bar charts than point and figure charts.

T   F   3. Trendlines and moving averages are typically not used with candlestick charts.

T   F   4. The main body of the candlestick line represents the range between the period's high and low prices.

T   F   5. A hammer pattern looks the same as a hanging man pattern.

T   F   6. A doji line occurs when the opening and closing prices for a period are the same.

Answers

1. *True.*
2. *True.*
3. *False.* Many technical analysis tools (including trendlines and moving averages) are commonly used in conjunction with candlestick charts.
4. *False.* The main body of the candlestick line represents the range between the period's opening and closing prices.
5. *True.*
6. *True.*

PUTTING IT ALL TOGETHER

THE WEIGHT-OF-EVIDENCE APPROACH TO TECHNICAL ANALYSIS

The first 18 lessons presented the basic, as well as some advanced, tools that the technician uses for market analysis. In this final lesson, these concepts will be tied together into a weight-of-evidence approach to technical analysis and demonstrated with three comprehensive real market examples.

On more than one occasion, I have had the opportunity to serve on a jury involving a criminal case. In each case, the prosecutor brought forth evidence suggesting the defendant's guilt, while the defense attorney presented facts supporting the defendant's innocence. After testimony was completed and closing statements were made, the judge charged myself and 11 others to evaluate all the facts presented and deliver a verdict of not guilty or guilty.

When examined in isolation, a given piece of evidence would indicate that the defendant was innocent, while another piece of evidence would imply guilt. However, our verdict was not based on just one or two isolated facts. Rather, it was based upon all of the evidence. Certain pieces of evidence were more convincing than others (based on our collective life experience) and, therefore, were given greater weight in reaching a verdict.

Reaching a not guilty or guilty verdict is in many ways analogous to deciding whether to buy or sell a security or market. Although a decision can be made on the basis of one piece of information, a better decision is normally made by examining multiple pieces of evidence.

As with the various pieces of evidence in a criminal case, each technical indicator's worth can be viewed differently when reaching a buy or sell decision. For example, penetration of a boundary line of a chart pattern that has developed over several months is recognized as being more significant than penetration of a trendline that has been in place for only a couple of weeks.

Always keep in mind that there is no technical indicator that is correct all of the time. Therefore, it is appropriate to examine multiple indicators and make buy and sell decisions based on the weight of evidence.

In this lesson, you are provided with three comprehensive real market examples of how to examine technical indicators in combination to reach a decision (buy, sell, or hold) based on the weight of evidence. For each of the examples, you are presented with technical evidence at a point in time from the following seven technical perspectives:

1. Charts patterns.
2. Trendlines.
3. Support and resistance.
4. Moving average crossover.
5. Envelopes.
6. Stochastics.
7. Moving Average Convergence-Divergence (MACD).

In addition, a conclusion regarding the weight of evidence at a point in time is given and compared to what actually happened thereafter. As you will note, examination of multiple indicators can be beneficial in determining the probable future direction of prices.

You should note that although seven different technical tools and indicators have been selected, others can be used in addition to or as substitutes for those presented. The primary objective is to show the benefit of using multiple indicators to gain a clear perspective of a security or market. There are many other indicators that can serve in that function with equal effectiveness.

TECHNICAL ANALYSIS TIP

When using multiple indicators, make sure that you use different types of indicators. Don't analyze similar types of indicators and assume you are examining a security or market from different perspectives. Be careful that the technical tools and indicators you use are not redundant and providing you with a biased picture of the security or market you are trading.

Example 1—Baxter International as of April 24, 2001

TECHNICAL EVIDENCE

Figures 19-1 through 19-7 provide a variety of technical perspectives on Baxter International as of April 24, 2001. Let's examine each for evidence.

Figure 19-1 (10-year bar chart using weekly data): Although some consolidation in prices did occur from early-1999 through mid-2000, the long-term trend is clearly up at this point in time.

Figure 19-2 (3-year bar chart using weekly data): Prices have moved sharply higher after completing a period of consolidation. The intermediate-term trend is up.

Figure 19-3 (6-month bar chart using daily data): Prices are moving higher along an up trendline. Minor resistance is noted at the $47.60 level. Nevertheless, the short-term trend must be viewed as positive until the up trendline is penetrated to the downside. A warning: Prices as of April 24 look like they may be forming a double top pattern. While you should certainly watch out for this pattern development, it is not unusual for prices to look like this in any security or market that is rising. In this case, penetration of the up trendline would be your first sign of a possible turnaround in the direction of prices from up to down.

Figure 19-4 (1-year bar chart using daily data with 20- and 50-day simple moving averages): The price of Baxter International as of April 24 is below both the 20- and 50-day simple moving averages. However, the last signal (buy) given by the shorter-term (20-day) simple moving average crossing above the longer-term (50-day) simple moving average remains in force and is a bullish sign.

Figure 19-5 (1-year bar chart using daily data with 6 percent envelopes around a 21-day simple moving average): Prices have moved between lower and upper envelope bands for the past six months and currently are about halfway between the 21-day simple moving average line and the lower envelope band. Although this may be interpreted as prices continuing within a well-defined uptrend, no strong signals are provided at this point in time.

Figure 19-6 (3-month bar chart using daily data with stochastics): Analysis of the stochastic indicator provides no clear clues as to future direction of prices. A bullish divergence may be starting to form, but more time is needed to know for sure.

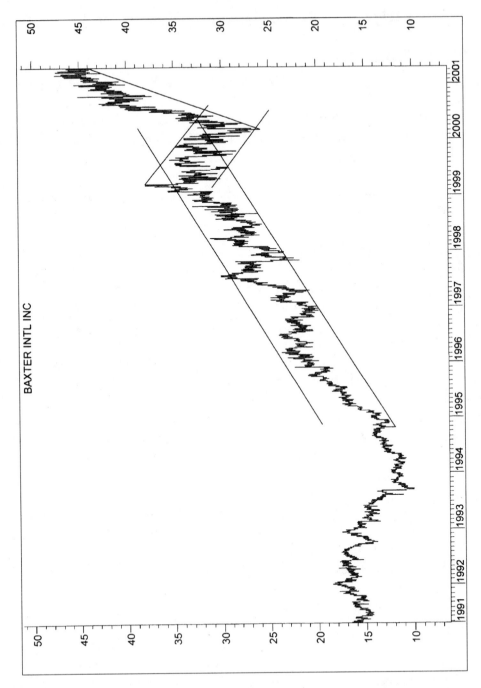

Figure 19-1   Long–Term Perspective for Baxter International as of April 24, 2001

238

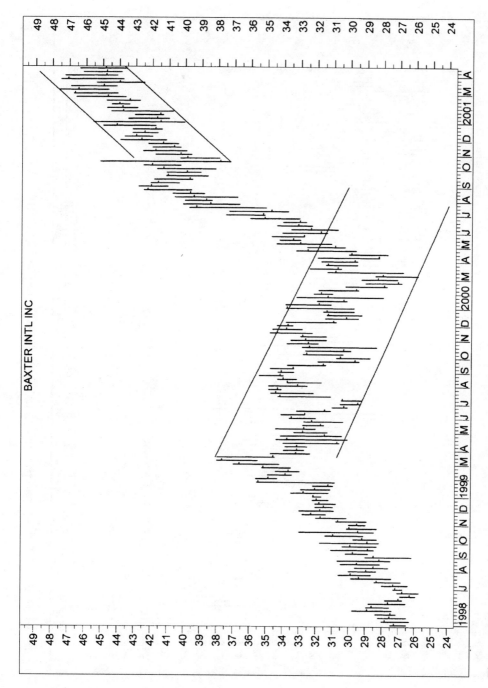

Figure 19-2   Intermediate-Term Perspective for Baxter International as of April 24, 2001

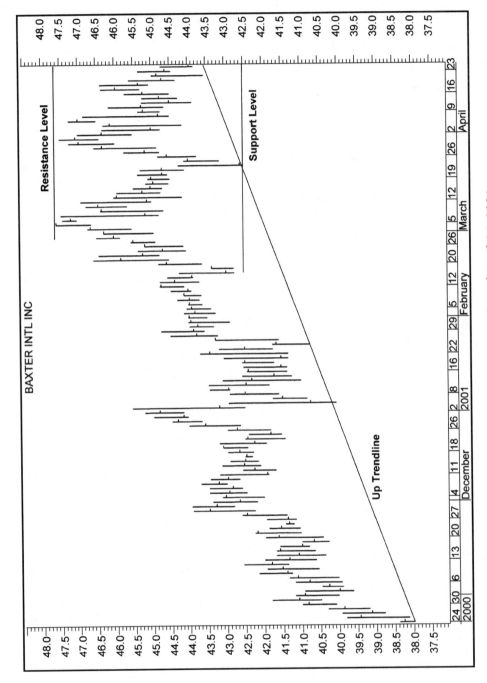

Figure 19-3   Short-Term Perspective for Baxter International as of April 24, 2001

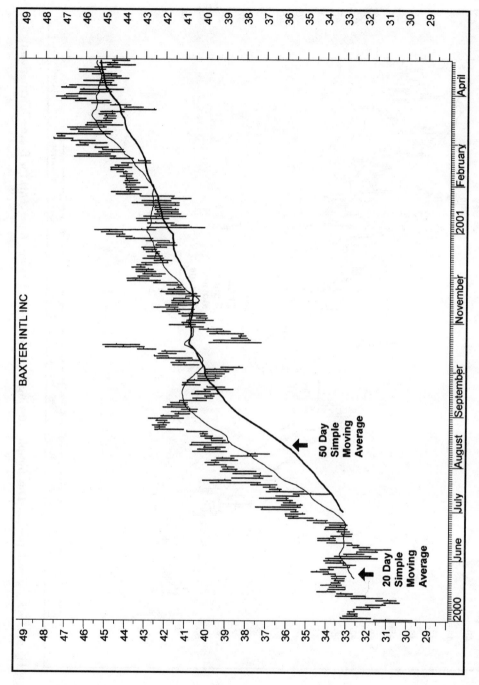

BAXTER INTL INC

50 Day Simple Moving Average

20 Day Simple Moving Average

Figure 19-4   The 20- and 50-Day Simple Moving Averages for Baxter International

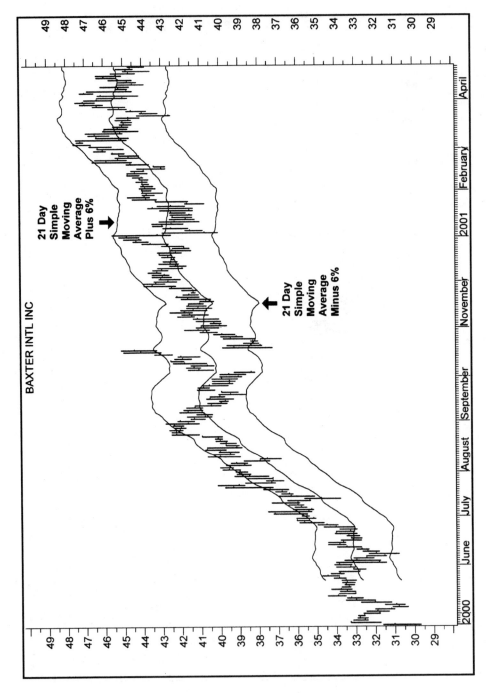

Figure 19-5 Envelopes (21-Day Simple Moving Average Plus and Minus 6 percent) for Baxter International

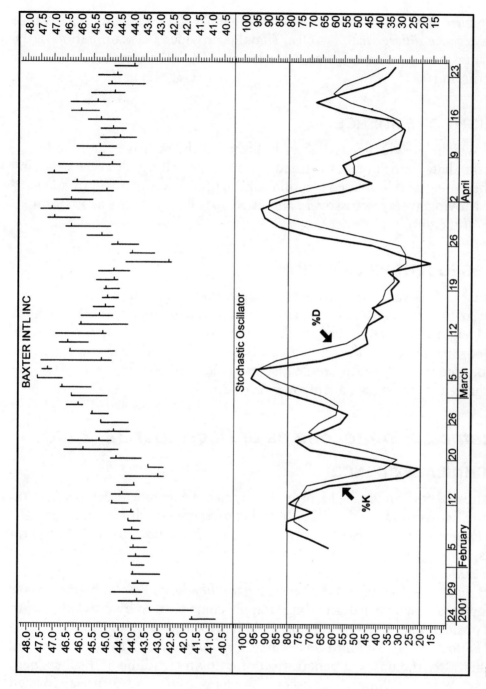

Figure 19-6   Five-Day Stochastics Plot for Baxter International

Figure 19-7 (6-month bar chart using daily data with moving average convergence-divergence): No clear signal is provided by examination of the moving average convergence-divergence (MACD) indicator for Baxter International.

WEIGHT OF EVIDENCE

The weight of evidence is clearly bullish. On the positive side, the long-, intermediate- and short-term trends in prices are all up. Prices are moving higher along a well-defined trendline and within a well-defined trend channel. Moving average crossovers and envelopes lend support to a continuation of the uptrend in prices.

SUBSEQUENT PRICE ACTION

Figure 19-8 (1-year bar chart using daily data) shows that prices found support at the up trendline on April 24 and moved higher thereafter just as the weight of evidence suggested. The up trendline continued to provide support for prices for the remainder of the time period shown on the chart. Also, note that the $47.60 resistance level identified on Figure 19-3 did act as short-term resistance again after April 24.

Example 2—AutoZone as of December 22, 2000

TECHNICAL EVIDENCE

Figures 19-9 through 19-15 provide a variety of technical perspectives on AutoZone as of December 22, 2000. Let's examine each for evidence.

Figure 19-9 (10-year bar chart using weekly data): From a long-term perspective, prices have essentially moved sideways from late 1993 through late 2000.

Figure 19-10 (3-year bar chart using weekly data): Prices appear to have completed a two-year descending triangle chart pattern by breaking out to the upside. Also, a strong support level has formed at about $21.

Figure 19-11 (6-month bar chart using daily data): Prices have moved higher after the upward penetration of a down trendline and subsequent retest. As prices climbed, an ascending triangle chart pattern was formed

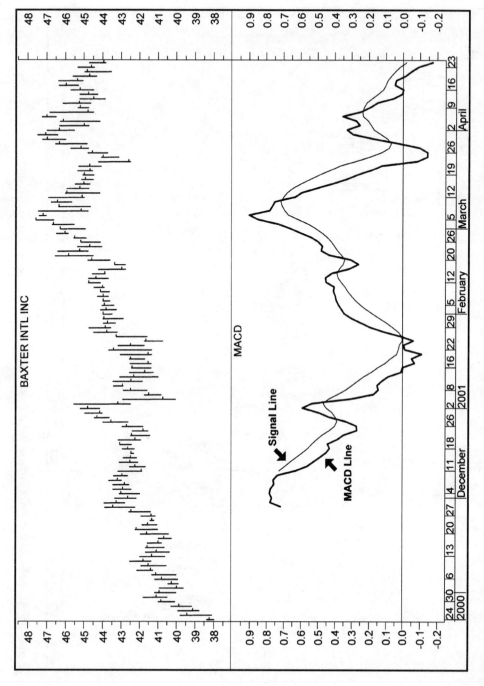

Figure 19-7   Moving Average Convergence-Divergence (MACD) for Baxter International

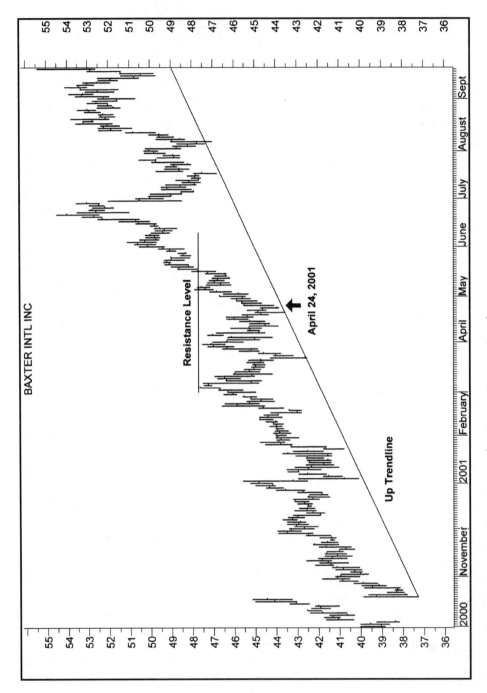

Figure 19-8   Subsequent Price Action for Baxter International

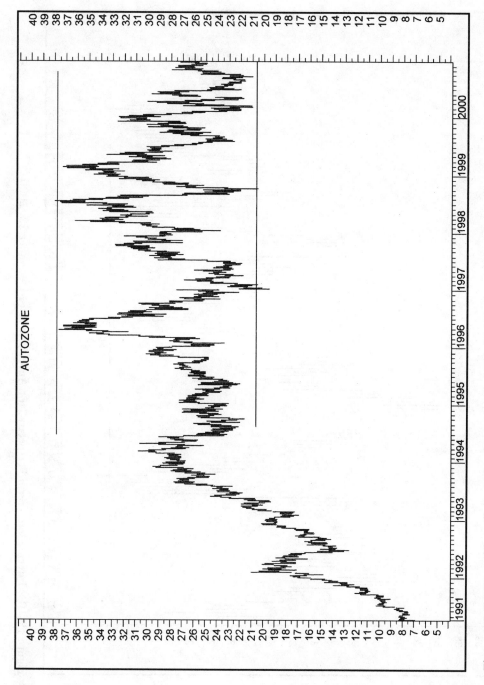

Figure 19-9   Long-Term Perspective for AutoZone as of December 22, 2000

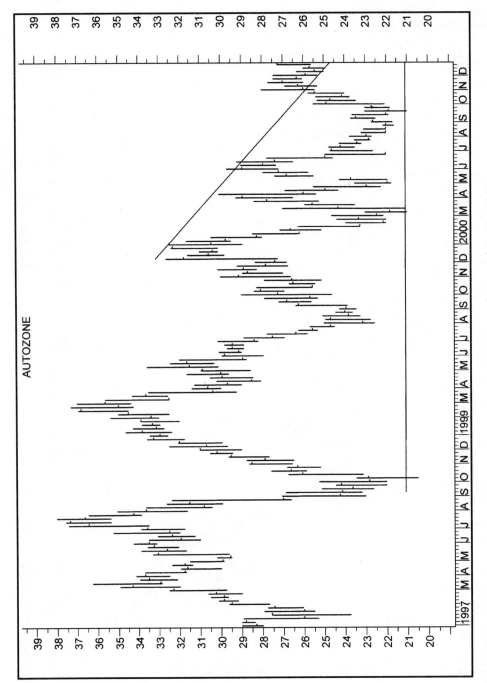

Figure 19-10 Intermediate-Term Perspective for AutoZone as of December 22, 2000

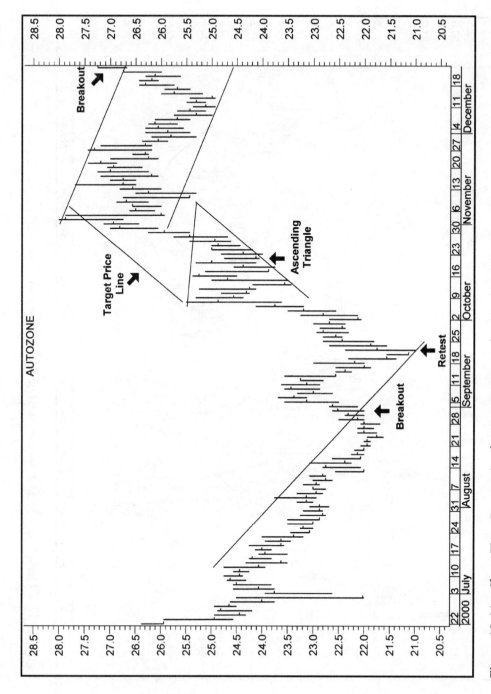

Figure 19-11   Short-Term Perspective for AutoZone as of December 22, 2000

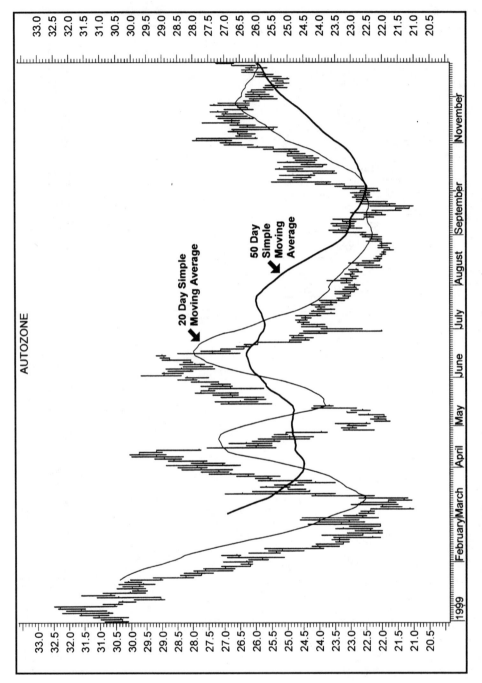

Figure 19-12   The 20- and 50-Day Simple Moving Averages for AutoZone

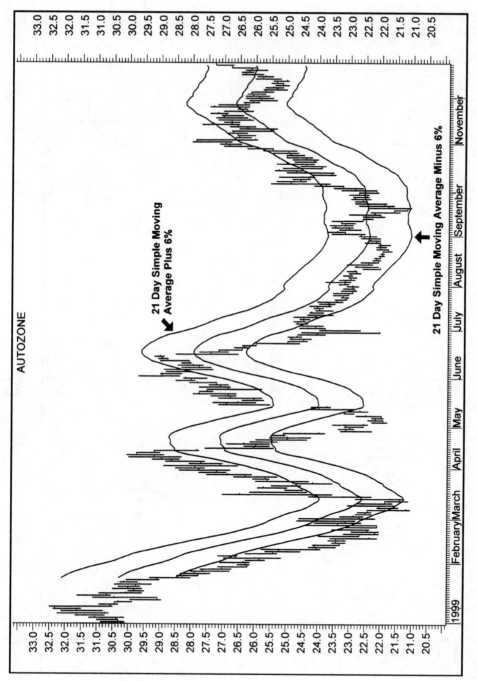

Figure 19-13   Envelopes (21-Day Simple Moving Average Plus and Minus 6 percent) for AutoZone

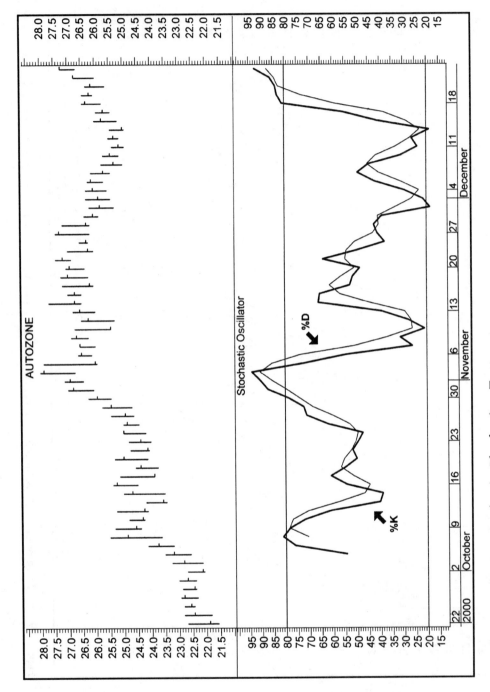

Figure 19-14   Five-Day Stochastics Plot for AutoZone

Figure 19-15 Moving Average Convergence-Divergence (MACD) for AutoZone

with prices reaching the target price indicated upon an upside breakout. Prices consolidated from late October through mid-December. An upside breakout of that consolidation pattern is noted on December 22.

Figure 19-12 (1-year bar chart using daily data with 20- and 50-day simple moving averages): The price of AutoZone as of December 22 is above both the 20- and 50-day simple moving averages. Although the two moving average lines are very close to each other, the last signal (buy) given by the shorter-term (20-day) simple moving average crossing above the longer-term (50-day) simple moving average remains in force and is a bullish sign.

Figure 19-13 (1-year bar chart using daily data with 6 percent envelopes around a 21-day simple moving average): Prices have been very volatile throughout the period charted and repeatedly have moved beyond both the upper and lower envelope bands. Prices are currently just inside the upper band.

Figure 19-14 (3-month bar chart using daily data with stochastics): Analysis of the stochastic indicator provides no clear clues as to future direction of prices.

Figure 19-15 (6-month bar chart using daily data with moving average convergence-divergence): No clear signal is provided by examination of the moving average convergence-divergence (MACD) indicator for AutoZone.

WEIGHT OF EVIDENCE

The weight of evidence in this case is mixed. As of December 22, the trend is sideways from a long-term perspective. The upside breakout of the descending triangle chart pattern on the intermediate-term chart (see Figure 19-10), combined with the penetration of the upper boundary line of a consolidation pattern on the short-term chart (see Figure 19-11), is bullish for the short- to intermediate-term time horizon. Furthermore, the lack of clear negative signals from the other technical indicators examined may be sufficient for some short-term traders to buy at this point. Risk adverse investors, including those with an intermediate- or long-term investing horizon, should clearly wait for more evidence before making a commitment.

TECHNICAL ANALYSIS TIP

The weight of evidence is often mixed when examining a particular security or market. A clear picture of what can be expected to hap-

pen to prices next does not always surface upon examination of a variety of technical indicators. Increase your probability of making successful investing decisions by being patient and waiting until the weight of evidence for the security or market that you are examining is compelling.

SUBSEQUENT PRICE ACTION

Figure 19-16 (1-year bar chart using daily data) shows that prices did move up for about three weeks after December 22, and nimble short-term traders may have been able to profit from a relatively quick trade. However, intermediate- and long-term investors would have been rewarded for their patience by waiting until late February 2001 to buy AutoZone. At that point in time, the weight of evidence was far more compelling and, subsequently, prices advanced sharply.

Example 3—Walt Disney as of June 14, 2001

TECHNICAL EVIDENCE

Figures 19-17 through 19-23 provide a variety of technical perspectives on Walt Disney as of June 14, 2001. Let's examine each for evidence.

Figure 19-17 (10-year bar chart using weekly data): Prices of Walt Disney have been in a gradual uptrend over the 10-year period shown, suggesting that the long-term trend is up at this point in time.

Figure 19-18 (3-year bar chart using weekly data): From an intermediate-term perspective, prices have been volatile with no clear direction noted.

Figure 19-19 (6-month bar chart using daily data): During late May and early June, prices penetrated a three-month uptrend channel to the downside, at first held at a support level (previous resistance changed to support), moved back to the lower boundary line of the uptrend channel, and, finally, broke below the support level. This price action is clearly bearish from a short-term perspective.

Figure 19-20 (1-year bar chart using daily data with 20- and 50-day simple moving averages): The price of Walt Disney as of June 14 is below both the 20- and 50-day simple moving averages. While the last signal (buy) given by the shorter-term (20-day) simple moving average crossing above the longer-term (50-day) simple moving average is still in force, note the

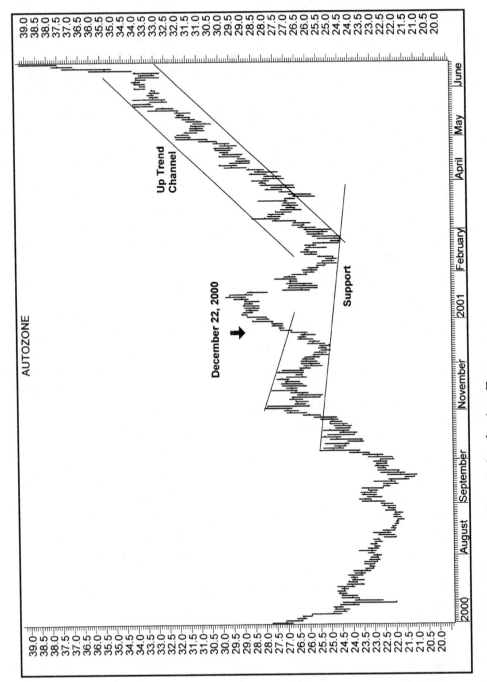

Figure 19-16   Subsequent Price Action for AutoZone

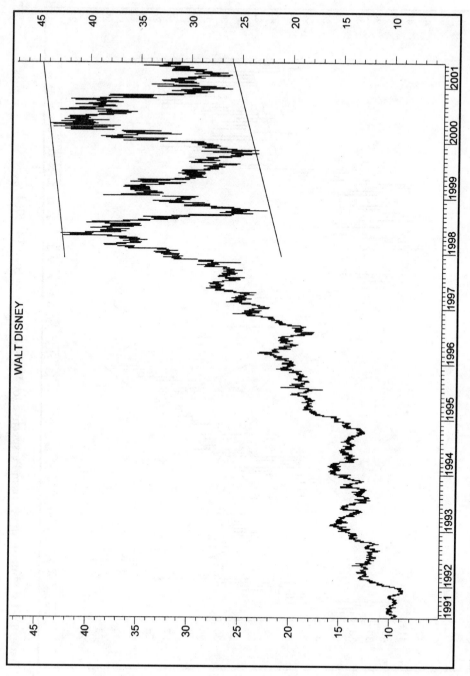

Figure 19-17   Long-Term Perspective for Walt Disney as of June 14, 2001

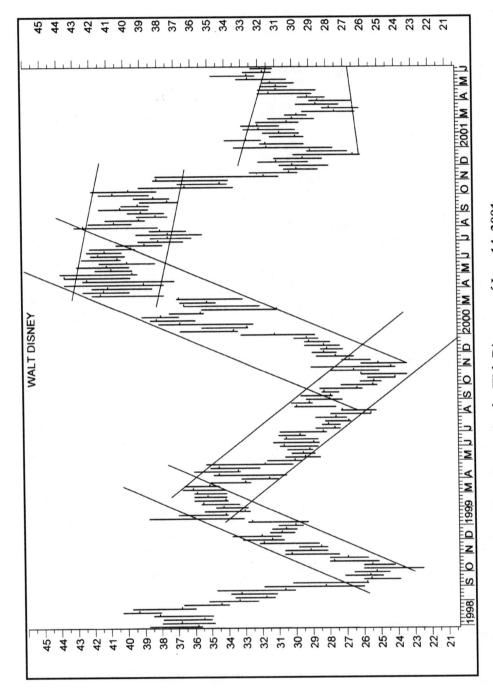

Figure 19-18   Intermediate-Term Perspective for Walt Disney as of June 14, 2001

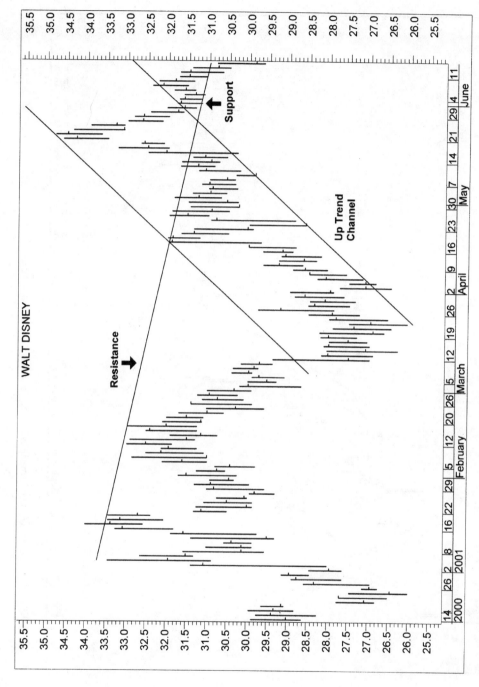

Figure 19-19   Short-Term Perspective for Walt Disney as of June 14, 2001

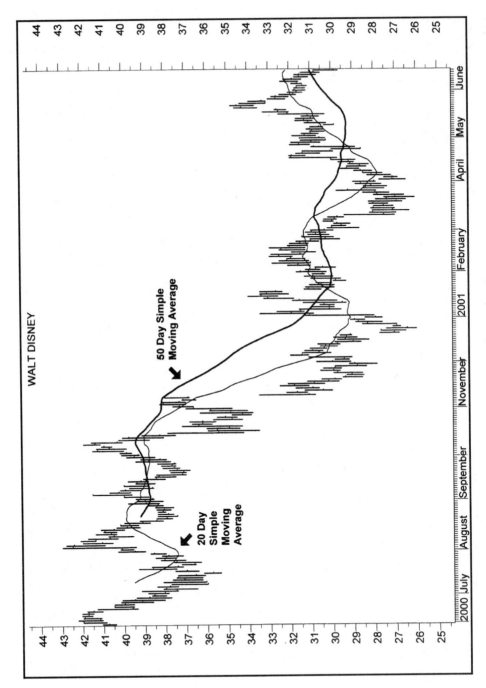

Figure 19-20   20- and 50-Day Simple Moving Averages for Walt Disney rapid decline in prices in late May and early June. Given the sharpness of the drop in prices, the two moving averages may soon cross over as old data (higher prices) drops out of the calculations and is replaced with more recent lower-priced data.

Figure 19-21 (1-year bar chart using daily data with 6 percent envelopes around a 21-day simple moving average): Prices have moved below the lower envelope band, suggesting lower prices to follow.

Figure 19-22 (3-month bar chart using daily data with stochastics): Analysis of the stochastic indicator provides no clear clues regarding the future direction of prices. A bullish divergence may be starting to form, but more time is needed to know for sure.

Figure 19-23 (6-month bar chart using daily data with moving average convergence-divergence): No clear signal is provided by examination of the moving average convergence-divergence (MACD) indicator for Walt Disney.

WEIGHT OF EVIDENCE

The weight of evidence suggests a bearish outlook for Walt Disney as of June 14, 2001. Short-term chart pattern analysis (see Figure 19-19) shows both uptrend channel penetration to the downside and prices falling below a support level. Further price weakness is indicated by prices falling below the lower envelope band (see Figure 19-21). With the intermediate-term picture uncertain and the long-term trend being only slightly up, this may turn out to be the start of a significant move downward in prices.

SUBSEQUENT PRICE ACTION

Figure 19-24 (1-year bar chart using daily data) shows that prices did, in fact, move significantly lower as suggested by the weight of evidence.

Final Thoughts

The best test of any investment approach is the test of time, and over many decades technical analysis has proven itself to be a valid and profitable approach to investing. As demonstrated in the previous real-market examples, when applied in a disciplined manner technical analysis works.

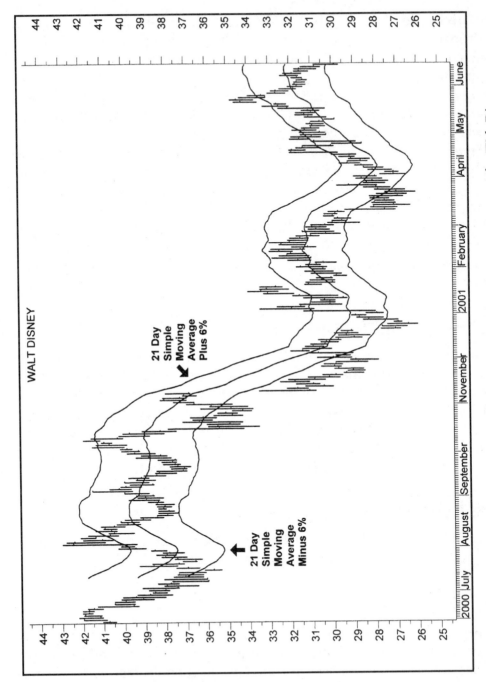

Figure 19-21   Envelopes (21-Day Simple Moving Average Plus and Minus 6 Percent) for Walt Disney

262

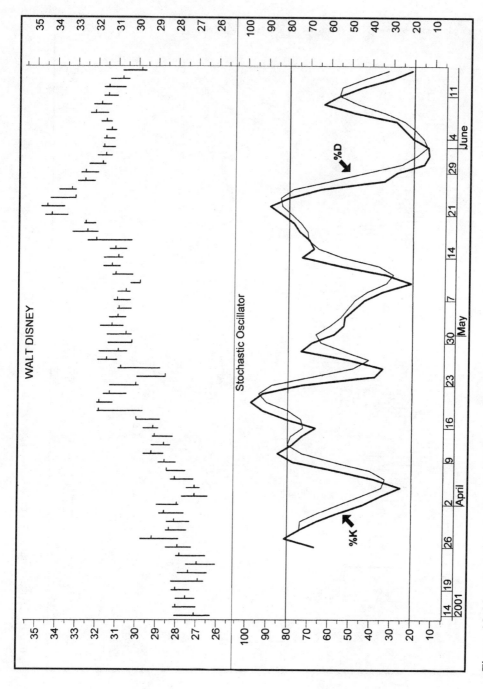

Figure 19-22   Five-Day Stochastics Plot for Walt Disney

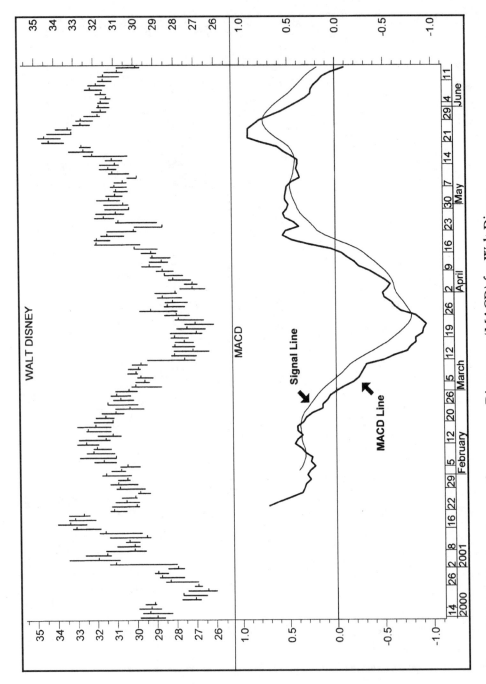

Figure 19-23   Moving Average Convergence-Divergence (MACD) for Walt Disney

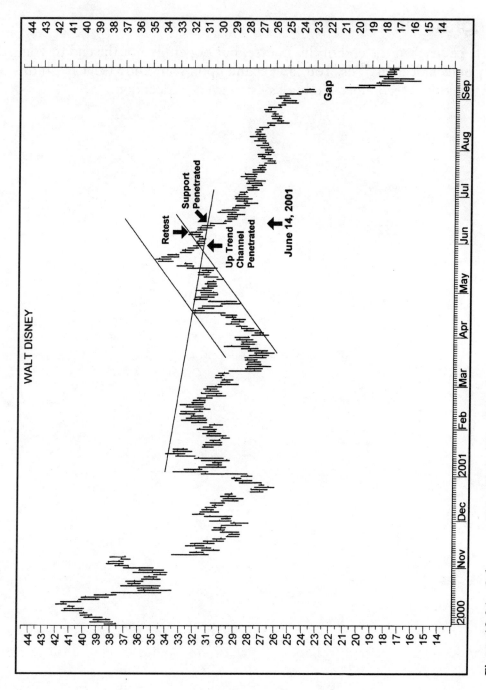

Figure 19-24   Subsequent Price Action for Walt Disney

Congratulations!

You have reached the end of this course, but hopefully not the end of your study of technical analysis. You can expand upon your knowledge by studying some of the recommended books listed in the Appendix.

APPENDIX

RECOMMENDED TECHNICAL ANALYSIS BOOKS

There is no question that books provide an excellent way to learn about new techniques and expand your knowledge of technical analysis at a relatively low cost. However, you must be careful when selecting books. Quite frankly, many technical analysis books provide little or no value. These books typically fall into the categories of (1) "get rich quick" trading systems that do not work in real-time trading, (2) those describing techniques in theoretical terms that cannot be practically implemented, and (3) books that are simply poorly written making it difficult to understand the material presented.

The good news is that the remaining books offer a wealth of valuable information. Some of these books were first published decades ago and have stood the test of time, while others have only recently been published.

For your benefit, the author has identified technical analysis books that are, in his opinion, the best. These books are organized alphabetically by title. After each title appears the book's author, number of pages in the book, copyright date, publisher's name, and a brief description of the book's contents.

The Arms Index (TRIN): An Introduction to the Volume Analysis of Stock and Bond Markets, Richard W. Arms, Jr., 100 pages, 1989, McGraw-Hill, New York, NY. Written by the originator of the Arms Index (commonly known as TRIN). Shows how to calculate and interpret the Arms Index in the stock and other markets. Presents numerous variations on the original Arms Index.

Bollinger on Bollinger Bands, John Bollinger, 226 pages, 2002, McGraw-Hill, New York, NY. Written by the originator of Bollinger Bands. Shows how to calculate and interpret Bollinger Bands.

A Complete Guide to the Futures Markets: Fundamental Analysis, Technical Analysis, Trading, Spreads, and Options, Jack D. Schwager, 741 pages, 1984, John Wiley & Sons, Inc., New York, NY. Primarily focuses on fundamental analysis. However, it also includes a good section on chart analysis and systems trading as applied to the futures markets.

Elliott Wave Principle: Key to Stock Market Profits (rev. ed.), Robert R. Prechter, Jr., and A. J. Frost, 249 pages, 1990, New Classics Library, Inc., Gainesville, GA. As the basic handbook of the Elliott Wave Principle, it is must reading for those interested in Elliott techniques. Thoroughly covers all the relevant concepts of the Elliott Wave Principle.

The Encyclopedia of Stock Market Techniques, Investors Intelligence, 744 pages, 1985, Investors Intelligence, New Rochelle, NY. Presents a wide variety of technical analysis concepts and approaches to the stock market. Each chapter is written by an expert on the topic discussed.

The Encyclopedia of Technical Market Indicators, Robert W. Colby and Thomas A. Meyers, 581 pages, 1988, McGraw-Hill, New York, NY. Presents the most comprehensive description of technical market indicators ever published. Representing thousands of hours of computerized research, it shows the true forecasting value of over 110 indicators.

Getting Started in Technical Analysis, Jack D. Schwager, 339 pages, 1999, John Wiley & Sons, Inc., New York, NY. Introductory level material is combined with market savvy commentary in this practical book.

How Charts Can Help You in the Stock Market, William L. Jiler, 202 pages, 1962 (reprinted in 1990), Fraser Publishing, Burlington, VT. Provides an excellent introduction to chart pattern analysis. Originally published in 1962 by Trendline (a division of Standard & Poor's Corporation).

Japanese Candlestick Charting Techniques: A Contemporary Guide to the Ancient Investment Techniques of the Far East, Steve Nison, 310 pages, 1991, New York Institute of Finance, New York, NY. Best for learning about Japanese candlestick charting. Teaches drawing and interpreting over 50 candlestick lines and formations. Shows how to use candlestick charting in conjunction with various other technical analysis techniques. Hundreds of real market examples are included.

The Japanese Chart of Charts, Seiki Shimizu, 206 pages, 1986, published by Tokyo Futures Trading Publishing Company, distributed by Windsor Books, Brightwaters, NY. An English translation of a Japanese book. Discusses origins of various Japanese charting methods. Presents the basics of candlestick chart construction. Describes numerous candlestick chart patterns to watch for and the proper way to interpret them. Finally, a variety of other chart related topics are discussed.

The Major Works of R. N. Elliott, Robert R. Prechter, Jr., Editor, 243 pages, 1980, New Classics Library, Inc., Gainesville, GA. Three ground-breaking works of Ralph Nelson Elliott are combined in this volume (The Wave Principle—1938; The Financial World—1939; and, Nature's Law—The Secret of the Universe—1946).

New Concepts in Technical Trading Systems, J. Welles Wilder, Jr., 141 pages, 1978, Trend Research, McLeansville, NC. This classic 1978 work presents several unique technical trading systems. It is the original source for the Relative Strength Index.

New Methods for Profit in the Stock Market, Garfield A. Drew, 384 pages, 1955, Fraser Publishing Company, Burlington, VT. Analyzes specific methods for stock market timing. Although originally published in 1955, the vast majority of concepts remains applicable to the stock market today.

Profits in the Stock Market, Harold M. Gartley, 446 pages, 1981, Traders Press Inc., Greenville, SC. A reprint of H. M. Gartley's 1935 classic on technical analysis. An outstanding supplemental package of charts is included. Particularly useful to those interested in studying stock market activity during the years before and after the great crash of 1929.

Technical Analysis Explained: The Successful Investor's Guide to Spotting Investment Trends and Turning Points (4th ed.), Martin J. Pring, 642 pages, 2002, McGraw-Hill, New York, NY. Presents a good overview of technical analysis basics and their application to various markets. Focuses on the relationships between interest rates and the stock market.

Technical Analysis from A to Z: Covers Every Trading Tool...From the Absolute Breadth Index to the Zig Zag (2d ed.), Steven B. Achelis, 380 pages, 2000, McGraw-Hill, New York, NY. Presents overviews, interpretations, and examples for over 135 technical indicators.

Technical Analysis of the Financial Markets: A Comprehensive Guide to Trading Methods and Applications, John J. Murphy, 542 pages, 1999, New York Institute of Finance, New York, NY. Provides comprehensive coverage of technical analysis techniques. Includes over 400 chart examples.

Technical Analysis of Stock Trends (8th ed.), Robert D. Edwards and John Magee, 709 pages, 2001, AMACOM, New York, NY. Many knowledgeable technicians consider this to be the best book on chart patterns ever written. Necessary reading for any serious student of technical analysis.

Technical Analysis of Stocks, Options & Futures: Advanced Trading Systems and Techniques, William F. Eng, 465 pages, 1988, McGraw-Hill, New York, NY. Examines 15 technical trading techniques. Explains the philosophy behind each technique. Shows how and when to use each of the 15 methods.

Three-Point Reversal Method of Point & Figure Construction and Formations, Michael L. Burke, 107 pages, 1990, Chartcraft, Inc., New Rochelle, NY. Essential reading for current-day point and figure chartists.

Trading Rules: Strategies for Success, William F. Eng, 266 pages, 1990, Dearborn Trade, Chicago, IL. A collection of 50 practical strategies for investing. Filled with proven principles that can lead to long-term trading profits.

Using Stochastics, Cycles & RSI, George C. Lane, 50 pages, 1986, Investment Educators, IL. Provides specific guidance on how to use stochastics, cycles, and RSI in a variety of markets. Written by the originator of stochastics.

Using Technical Analysis: A Step-by-Step Guide to Understanding and Applying Stock Market Charting Techniques (rev. ed.), Clifford Pistolese, 252 pages, 1994, McGraw-Hill, New York, NY. Identifies chart patterns to watch for and how to interpret them.

Volume Cycles in the Stock Market: Market Timing through Equivolume Charting, Richard W. Arms, Jr., 141 pages, 1983, Business One Irwin, Homewood, IL. Describes how Arms uses trading volume to forecast price changes. Stresses that price change cycles are not influenced by the times, but by the trading volume of the stock market. Two original concepts, Volume Cyclicality and Ease of Movement, are explained in detail and their relationships to Equivolume charting are shown.

Winning Market Systems, Gerald Appel, 231 pages, 1989, Windsor Books, Brightwaters, NY. An excellent collection of stock market related trading ideas.

GLOSSARY

Accumulation   Occurs when the supply of a security is less than the demand.

Bar chart   A chart of price versus time. The vertical axis indicates price; time intervals are marked on the horizontal axis. For each time period, a vertical line denotes the high and low price of the security; a short horizontal protrusion to the right of the vertical line shows the closing price.

Bearish   The belief that market prices will decline.

Bear market   A market when prices are declining.

Bottom   A low for a security or the overall market.

Breadth   The number of stocks advancing minus those declining. When the number of advancing issues exceeds the number of declining issues, the breadth of the market is viewed as bullish. On the other hand, when the number of advancing issues is less than the number of declining issues, breadth is considered to be a bearish sign.

Breakout   A substantial rise in price above a resistance level or decline in price below a support level. When a breakout occurs, a price trend is likely to continue.

Bullish   The belief that market prices will rise.

Bull market   A market when prices are rising.

Buying climax   A sharp price run-up accompanied by extremely high volume created by investors rushing in to buy securities. This often happens at the end of an up price movement and typically represents a good time to sell.

Channel   A trading range between two parallel lines in which prices move. The slope of the channel represents the direction of the trend.

Confirmation   Refers to the comparison of two or more technical indicators to ensure that they are pointing in the same direction and confirming one another.

Congestion area   A sideways trading range where supply and demand balance out.

Consolidation area   A trading range in which prices move until continuing in the same direction as the trend prior to the consolidation area.

Contrary opinion   A belief opposite of the general public and Wall Street professionals. At major market turning points, the overall consensus of opinion regarding the future direction of security prices is usually wrong. Thus, an investor taking a contrary view can profit at those times.

Correction   When prices move in the opposite direction of a major trend.

Cycle   A price pattern of movement that regularly occurs in a given time interval.

Distribution   Occurs when the demand for a security is less than the supply.

Divergence   Divergence is the opposite of confirmation. It occurs when one indicator points in one direction (such as, up) and another indicator points in another direction (such as, down).

Downtrend   When the price of a security or the overall market is declining.

Envelope   Contains normal price fluctuations. It is shown graphically as parallel lines at certain percentage points above and below a graph of an indicator or study. If the price goes outside the band, the strength or weakness of the trend is extraordinary. Also known as a trading band.

Exhaustion   When buying power is no longer enough to move prices up or when selling power is no longer enough to move prices lower.

False breakout   A breakout of a chart pattern that aborts. To ensure that a breakout is genuine, look for confirmation by the same or other indicators.

Fundamental analysis   An analytical technique for the buying and selling of stocks based on the belief that stock prices are determined by the underlying value of a company in terms of its cash, current assets, and earnings.

Gap   Represents a price range on a chart at which no trading takes place. When a gap occurs in an uptrend, the current period's low is higher than the previous period's high. In a downtrend, a gap appears when the current period's high is lower than the previous period's low.

Momentum   The rate of expansion of a security's price or volume.

Moving average   A tool used to smooth price fluctuations, allowing you to better determine price trends.

Moving average, exponential   Calculated by multiplying the difference between the current period's price and the exponential moving average for the previous period by an exponent, which varies depending on the length of the moving average. You then add the product of that calculation to the previous exponential moving average to arrive at the current period's exponential moving average.

Moving average, simple   Calculated by adding data for a set period of time and dividing the total by the number of periods.

Moving average, weighted   Calculated by averaging data over a set period of time, giving more emphasis to the most recent data.

On-balance volume (OBV)   A technical indicator that manipulates volume figures. If the stock price falls to a new low and the OBV does not, the indicator is interpreted as being a positive sign; if the stock price rises to a new high and the OBV does not, the indicator is interpreted as being negative.

Optimization   A test performed on historical data to determine what would have resulted in the maximum profit during a given period of time.

Option   The right to buy or sell specific securities at a specified price within a specified time. A call option gives the holder the right to buy; a put option gives the holder the right to sell.

Overbought   The point (after a period of vigorous buying) at which upward momentum in prices can no longer be maintained and prices can be expected to stabilize or decline.

Oversold   The opposite of overbought. It is a point at which downward momentum in prices can no longer be maintained and prices can be expected to remain stable or rise.

Point and figure chart   Records price activity without reference to time and volume. These charts are used to determine the trend in a security's price.

Price objective   The technical appraisal of a security's future value.

Primary trend   The predominant movement of a market (stock, bond, commodity, or other). When it is up, it is known as a bull market. When it is down, it is called a bear market.

Pullback   When a security or the overall market falls back from a previous advance.

Rally   A brisk advance following a decline in prices.

Reaction   A temporary decline following an advance in prices.

Relative strength   A comparison of the performance of two items, such as an individual stock or group of stocks to the overall market. Relative strength analysis helps select stocks that are likely to outperform the overall market.

Resistance level   The price at which sellers tend to sell in sufficient volume to lower the price of a security. For example, if on a few occasions the price of a given stock has risen to around $50 per share and, on each occasion, the price has subsequently dropped, a technical analyst would consider $50 per share to be a resistance level for that stock.

Secondary trend   Market movement in the opposite direction of the primary trend. These are temporary interruptions in a bull or bear market.

Selling climax   A sharp price decline accompanied by extremely high volume created by panic stricken investors dumping securities. This often happens at the end of a bear market and typically represents a good time to buy.

Short covering   The process of buying stock to close out a short sale.

Short selling   Selling stock not owned in anticipation of buying it back later at a lower price for a profit.

Support level   The price at which buyers tend to buy in sufficient volume to raise the price of a given security. For example, if on a few occasions the price of a given stock has dropped to around $25 per share and, on each occasion, the price has subsequently risen, a technical analyst would consider $25 per share to be a support level for that stock.

Technical analysis   The study of stocks and the overall market based on supply and demand. Technical analysts use charts of historical price and volume activity to predict future price movements.

Technician   One who employs technical analysis as a basis for investment decisions.

Top   A high for a security or the overall market.

Trader   One who buys or sells securities for short-term profits.

Trend   The trend is the direction of a price movement.

Trendline   A straight line on a chart that connects consecutive tops or consecutive bottoms of prices. Trendlines are used to identify levels of support and resistance.

Uptrend   When the price of a security or the overall market is rising.

Volume   The number of shares traded in a security or a market during a period (such as, a day or week).

Volume histogram   Usually accompanies a high-low-close bar chart. Volume is shown at the bottom of the chart by a vertical bar under each period's price data.

Whipsaw   Occurs when the technique that a trader is using produces many buy and sell signals in a small price range that do not follow through in the predicted direction. Whipsaw trades cause the trader to lose money.

INDEX

About the Author

Thomas A. Meyers is a recognized authority on using computers for investment research and analysis. Meyers has been quoted frequently by financial and business publications such as *Business Week, Investor's Business Daily, Forbes,* and *The New York Times*. He is the author of more than 100 articles on the subject of investing and coauthor of the highly acclaimed *Encyclopedia of Technical Market Indicators*.